Payment Systems in Global Perspective

Using information collected from central banks in 70 countries, this book, published in association with the Bank of England's Centre for Central Banking Studies, examines the development of payment instruments and payment systems in industrial, transitional and developing economies. The book starts by examining the availability and use of alternative payment instruments before analysing the development of payment systems and comparing relevant features of alternative systems; the recent adoption of real-time gross settlement systems in industrial, transitional and developing countries raises many interesting questions of design. The book then considers the relative importance of different types of payment risks during this development process and how payment system design affects these risks. Because failure in the payment system can produce a domino effect, these and other externalities provide the main justification for central bank intervention. Payment systems are also important from the central bank's perspective in that they impinge in various ways on monetary policy and financial stability. So the book then analyses the linkages between payment system policies, on the one hand, and monetary policy and financial stability, on the other.

Maxwell J. Fry is Director of the Bank of England's Centre for Central Banking Studies and holds the Chair in International Finance at the University of Birmingham. **Isaack Kilato** is Director of the National Payment System Improvement Project at the Bank of Tanzania. **Sandra Roger** is a Project Analyst at the Bank of England's Centre for Central Banking Studies. **Krzysztof Senderowicz** is Deputy Director of the National Bank of Poland's Payment Systems Department. **David Sheppard** is an Adviser in the Bank of England's Payment and Settlement Policy Division. **Francisco Solis** is Payment System Manager at the Banco de México. **John Trundle** is Head of the Bank of England's Payment and Settlement Policy Division.

Routledge International Studies in Money and Banking

1. *Private Banking in Europe*
   Lyn Bicker
2. *Bank Deregulation and Monetary Order*
   George Selgin
3. *Money in Islam: A Study in Islamic Political Economy*
   Masudul Alam Choudhury
4. *The Future of European Financial Centres*
   Kirsten Bindemann
5. *Payment Systems in Global Perspective*
   Maxwell J. Fry, Isaack Kilato, Sandra Roger, Krzysztof Senderowicz, David Sheppard, Francisco Solis, John Trundle

Payment Systems in Global Perspective

Maxwell J. Fry, Isaack Kilato, Sandra Roger, Krzysztof Senderowicz, David Sheppard, Francisco Solis, John Trundle

Foreword by Eddie George
Governor of the Bank of England

Published in association with the Bank of England's Centre for Central Banking Studies

London and New York

First published 1999
by Routledge
11 New Fetter Lane, London EC4P 4EE

Simultaneously published in the USA and Canada
by Routledge
29 West 35th Street, New York, NY 10001

Typeset in New Times Roman by Maxwell Fry using Leslie Lamport's LaTeX, a set of macros for Donald Knuth's TeX typesetting software.

Printed and bound in Great Britain by
T. J. International Ltd., Padstow, Cornwall

British Library Cataloguing in Publication Data
A catalogue record for this book is available from the British Library

Library of Congress Cataloging in Publication Data
A catalogue record for this book has been requested

ISBN 0–415–20764–9 (hbk)

Contents

Figures

Tables

Authors

Maxwell J. Fry, Director of the Bank of England's Centre for Central Banking Studies and Professor of International Finance at the University of Birmingham, took BSc and PhD degrees at the London School of Economics. Maxwell lived and worked abroad for 20 years—in Afghanistan, France, Portugal, Turkey and the United States—before returning to the United Kingdom in 1989. Consulting assignments in some 40 countries, as well as with the international agencies, have provided the practical experience on which much of his academic work is based. Over the past 30 years, Maxwell has published over 200 articles and a dozen books. He is well known internationally for his work on money, interest and banking in economic development.

Isaack Kilato took a BA in economics and statistics at the University of Dar es Salaam before he was recruited to the Bank of Tanzania as an Economist in the Research Department. After joining the Bank but before his promotion to Senior Economist, Isaack took an MA in monetary economics at the University of Dar es Salaam. At the Bank of Tanzania, Isaack has held appointments as Director of Import Licensing (1986), Director of Exchange Control (1990), Director of Banking (1994) and Director of Financial Markets (1997). He is now the Director of the National Payment System Improvement Project in Tanzania, currently managed by the Bank of Tanzania.

Sandra Roger graduated in economics and finance from the University of Orleans and received an MSc in money, banking and finance from the University of Birmingham before joining the Bank of England's Centre for Central Banking Studies as Project Analyst in 1997. As a member of the project team that undertook the research for this book, Sandra was responsible for collating and analysing the questionnaire responses.

Krzysztof Senderowicz received a Bachelor's degree in economics from the Central School of Planning and Statistics in Warsaw and a Master's degree in finance and statistics from the Warsaw School of Economics before joining the National Bank of Poland's Research Department in 1989. Since 1992, Krzysztof has been working on the development of Polish payment and settlement systems. As Deputy Director of the Bank's Payment Systems Department, he is responsible for the introduction of a real-time gross settlement system in Poland.

David Sheppard, Adviser in the Bank of England's Payment and Settlement Policy Division, has worked on payment system policies since 1989. Responsible for the Bank of England's provision of training and technical assistance on payment systems since 1992, David has run courses in the United Kingdom, most countries in Central/Eastern Europe and Russia, where he was also a member of the International Monetary Fund's team advising the central bank. Recently, he has worked with the European Central Bank and the other European Union central banks in assessing the compliance of particular payment systems with the agreed risk management standards.

Francisco Solis studied mathematics at the Universities of Yucatán and Kentucky. He joined the Banco de México in 1981 as a researcher and project coordinator. Francisco's interest in payment and settlement system issues started in 1992, when he designed and led the development of a queue-processing scheme for a securities settlement system. In 1994 he became involved in the reform of the Mexican payment system. As Payment System Manager, Francisco is responsible for risk assessment and new developments in Mexico's payment system.

John Trundle graduated from Cambridge University in economics and holds an MBA from the London Business School/Wharton School before joining the Bank of England. At the Bank, he has worked on monetary policy, banking operations and market trading structures and settlement arrangements. As Head of the Bank's Payment and Settlement Policy Division, John's responsibilities cover payment arrangements, electronic money, foreign exchange settlement, securities and derivatives settlement, as well as policy issues raised by the Year 2000 problem. He is a member of the G-10's Committee on Payment and Settlement Systems and of the equivalent committee at the European Central Bank that guides the TARGET project. John chairs the G-10 working group set up to consider the establishment of core principles for payment systems.

Foreword

In June 1998 the Bank of England hosted its fifth Central Bank Governors' Symposium. As an innovation for this fifth Symposium, I asked the Bank's Centre for Central Banking Studies to prepare a report based on a workshop on payment and settlement systems held in January 1998 that was attended by staff from 22 central banks. This workshop was followed up by a three-month project involving specialist staff from the central banks of Mexico, Poland and Tanzania, as well as from the Bank of England—the authors of this book. In addition, as part of this project, survey data on payment systems were collected from 70 central banks representing a wide range of developed, transitional and developing economies—a first I believe.

The Bank's first Symposium was held in 1994, when more than 130 central bank governors and former governors gathered to mark the Bank of England's tercentenary. In keeping with the occasion, the papers concentrated primarily on the history and circumstances of central banks in the industrialised countries (Capie, Goodhart, Fischer and Schnadt 1994). To complement that book, a report on central banking in developing countries was produced for the second Symposium held during the 1995 meeting of governors (Fry, Goodhart and Almeida 1996).

Among other things, the analysis presented at the second Symposium found that inflation was *positively* related to the proportion of government borrowing from the central bank and in total domestic credit; and that inflation was *negatively* related to growth. The findings raised the questions: how should a government best meet its borrowing requirements and what roles might central banks usefully play? These were the issues addressed at our 1996 Symposium when concentrating on specific central banking issues enabled us to share experiences in considerably greater depth (Fry 1997). Following this practice, the 1997

Symposium report focused on financial regulation (Goodhart, Hartmann, Llewellyn, Rojas-Suárez and Weisbrod 1998).

Payment systems represent the financial plumbing of an economy and, as such, they tend to be noticed only when they go wrong. But the values of flows through many payment systems have now become so large that problems in them could cause serious disruptions to business and lead to financial instability. This is one reason why central banks take a close interest in payment systems and, indeed, many of them operate their country's main payment system. Moreover, we are currently seeing some important changes in this field, including the launch at the beginning of 1999 by the European Central Bank and the EU national central banks of TARGET, a cross-border real-time gross settlement system for payments in euro.

Payment systems are not however just a matter for central bank technicians; central bank governors need to understand the issues raised in the design and management of payment systems so that they can oversee their central banks' payments strategy and operations. At the 1998 Symposium, we discussed in particular risk and efficiency aspects of payment arrangements. Several governors admitted that they needed to know more about these issues. I hope, therefore, that the publication of this book, which extends the Symposium report, will play a part in increasing our understanding of payment issues in a range of different country environments. Because of the rapid growth in cross-border payments, it is in everyone's interests to be aware of payment systems in a global perspective.

Eddie George
Governor of the Bank of England

Acknowledgements

FIRST AND FOREMOST, our thanks go to the 70 central banks that kindly responded to the questionnaire reproduced in Appendix 1; much of our analysis is based on these questionnaire responses. Several central bank governors made useful remarks on the project report, on which this book is based, prepared for the Bank of England's Central Bank Governors' Symposium in June 1998. We are particularly grateful to the discussants at the Symposium—Ryszard Kokoszczynksi (National Bank of Poland), Idris Rashidi (Bank of Tanzania) and Gordon Thiessen (Bank of Canada)—for their extensive comments. We are also indebted to John Gubert (HSBC Holdings), Peter Howells (University of East London), Kent Matthews (Cardiff Business School), two anonymous referees and, at the Bank of England, Bill Allen, John Footman, Robert Heath, Joanna Place and Gabriel Sterne for suggestions on earlier drafts of this book.

As part of this project, Seneti 'Aho (National Reserve Bank of Tonga) undertook an initial cross-country analysis of velocity and inflation. At the Bank of England, Eddie George provided perceptive insights into the market mechanisms linking payment systems and foreign exchange markets, Lavan Mahadeva expedited the questionnaire analysis, Emma McDonnell interpreted the myriad acronyms in the payments literature, Helena Skarbek assisted the project team in diverse ways and Richard Wellington explained the practical issues involved in converting a deferred net settlement system into a real-time gross settlement system. Kath Begley, Christine Chaplin, Lucy Clary, Tony Ison, Debbie Nyman, Howard Picton, Kathryn Stones and Lorraine Yuille provided outstanding administrative, bibliographical, secretarial and technical support. At Routledge, Alison Kirk and Sally Carter gave much encouragement and highly skilled guidance. Christine Firth (Editorial Services, Checkendon, Oxon) copy-edited the manuscript and Dina Dineva (Editorial Services, Annapolis, Md) prepared the index.

During the January 1998 workshop, Peter Allsopp, Hans Blommestein (Organisation for Economic Co-operation and Development), Richard Dale (University of Southampton), Robert Effros (International Monetary Fund), Jean-Michel Godeffroy (European Monetary Institute), John Gubert, Omotunde Johnson (International Monetary Fund), Robert Keppler (World Bank), Brian Larkman (National Westminster Bank), Michael Lewis (Association for Payment Clearing Services), Robert Lindley (Bank for International Settlements), Heidi Richards (Board of Governors of the Federal Reserve System) and Bruce Summers (Federal Reserve Automation Services) gave insightful presentations on specific issues arising in payment system policies that set the stage for our follow-up project.

At the Bank for International Settlements, Claudio Borio, Andrew Crockett, Charles Freeland, Gregor Heinrich, Laurent Sahuquet and, particularly, Paul Van den Bergh provided helpful guidance at the preparatory stages of organising the academic workshop and project at the Bank of England's Centre for Central Banking Studies. We also received assistance at this planning stage from Allen Berger, Diana Hancock, Oliver Ireland, Jeffrey Marquardt, Bruce Summers, all at the Federal Reserve System, Mario Blejer, Robert Effros, Jeffery Gable, Manuel Guitián, Alfredo Leone, Garry Schinasi, Gabriel Sensenbrenner, at the International Monetary Fund, Jonathan Fiechter, Tom Glaessner, Robert Keppler, David Wilton, at the World Bank, Ramesh Basant Roi (Bank of Mauritius) and Liliana Rojas-Suárez (Deutsche Morgan Grenfell).

The views expressed in this book do not necessarily reflect those of the Bank of England or any individual acknowledged above. All errors remain the sole responsibility of the authors.

Acronyms

ACH	Automated clearing house
ACO	Athens Clearing Office
ACSS	Automated Clearing Settlement System (Canada)
APACS	Association for Payment Clearing Services (London)
APCA	Australian Payment Clearing Association
ARTIS	Austrian Real Time Interbank Settlement
ATM	Automated teller machine
BI-REL	Banca d'Italia Regolamento Lordo
BIS	Bank for International Settlements
BISC	Belarus Interbank Settlement Center
BISERA	Banking Integrated System for Electronic Transfers (Bulgaria)
BITS	Bank Interchange and Transfer System
BoE	Bank of England
BoF	Bank of Finland
BoK	Bank of Korea
CBR	Central Bank of Russia
CHAPS	Clearing House Automated Payment System (London)
CHATS	Clearing House Automated Transfer System (Hong Kong)
CHIPS	Clearing House Interbank Payments System (New York)
CISP	Interbank Coordinating Commission for the Retail Payment System (Portugal)
CNAPS	China National Advanced Payment System
COMPE	Multilateral Clearing System for Cheques and Remittance Documents (Brazil)
CPA	Canadian Payment Association
CRI	Interbank Settlement Committee (France)

CSC	Cash and Settlement Centre (Russia)
CSD	Central securities depository
DNS	Deferred net settlement
DVP	Delivery versus payment
EAF	Euro Access Frankfurt
EBA	Euro Banking Association
ECB	European Central Bank
ECCB	Eastern Caribbean Central Bank
ECHO	Exchange Clearing House Organisation (London)
EFTS	Electronic Funds Transfer System
EIS	Electronic Interbank System (China)
ELLIPS	Electronic Large-Value Interbank Payment System (Belgium)
ELS	Euro Link System (Frankfurt)
EMI	European Monetary Institute
EMU	European Monetary Union
EU	European Union
G-10	Group of Ten (actually 11 countries—Belgium, Canada, France, Germany, Italy, Japan, Netherlands, Sweden, Switzerland, United Kingdom and United States)
GDP	Gross domestic product
HBA	Hellenic Bank Association (Greece)
HERMES	Hellenic Real-time Money transfer Express System (Greece)
HKAB	Hong Kong Association of Banks
HKMA	Hong Kong Monetary Authority
IGS	Interbank Giro System (Hungary)
IMF	International Monetary Fund (Washington, DC)
KTFC	Korea Financial Telecommunications and Clearings Institute
LIFFE	London International Financial Futures and Options Exchange
LVTS	Large-value transfer system
MAS	Monetary Authority of Singapore
MEPS	MAS Electronic Payment System
NBP	National Bank of Poland
NBS	National Bank of Slovakia
NCH	National Clearing House (Poland)
NIBSS	Nigeria Inter-Bank Settlement System

NIFT	National Institutional Facilitation Technology (Pakistan)
NPC	National Payment(s) Council
PAR	Prime Assets Requirement (Australia)
PBC	People's Bank of China
PDS	Payment Delivery System (Australia)
POPS	Banks' On-line Express Transfer and Cheque System (Finland)
PVP	Payment versus payment
QM	Quasi-money
RBA	Reserve Bank of Australia
Repo	Repurchase agreement
RITS	Reserve Bank Information and Transfer System (Australia)
RIX	Clearing and Interbank System (Sweden)
RTGS	Real-time gross settlement
SADC	South African Development Community
SAMA	Saudi Arabian Monetary Agency
SAMOS	South African Multiple Option Settlement
SARIE	Saudi Arabian Riyal Interbank Express
SEBRA	Banco de la República Electronic Services (Colombia)
SEPI	Servicio Español de Pagos Interbancarios
SHIFT	System for Handling Interbank Funds Transfers (Singapore)
SIAC	Sistema de Informació a Cuentahabientes (Mexico)
SIBS	Interbank Services Company (Portugal)
SIC	Swiss Interbank Clearing
SIPS	Slovak Interbank Payment System
SLBE	Servicio de Liquidacion del Banco de España
SNB	Swiss National Bank
SNCC	Slovak National Clearing Centre
SNP	Système Net Protégé (France)
SPEEDS	Electronic Funds and Securities Transfer System (Malaysia)
SPEUA	Sistema de Pagos Electrónicos de Uso Ampliado (Mexico)
SPGT	Sistema de Pagamentos de Grandes Transacções (Portugal)
SVTS	Small-value transfer system

SWIFT	Society for Worldwide International Financial Telecommunications
TARGET	Trans-European Automated Real-time Gross settlement Express Transfer system
TBF	Transferts Banque de France
TIC-RTGS	Turkish Interbank Clearing System
TVM	Time value of money
VSAT	Very small aperture satellite terminal

Chapter 1

Introduction

INFORMATION ON PAYMENTS ARRANGEMENTS in transitional and developing countries is both scarce and not generally available in a form suitable for comparative analysis.[1] So in January 1998, the Bank of England asked central banks in a sample of countries, hereafter referred to as the BoE group, to complete a questionnaire both to supplement published information and to supply comparative data for analytical purposes.[2] The questionnaire responses provide new statistical and institutional information that we report and analyse in this study, from central bankers' perspectives, of selected aspects of payment systems in industrial, transitional and developing countries. As we did not choose the 70 respondent countries listed in Table 1.1 at random, they are not necessarily representative. We chose them because members of their central banks attended conferences on payment systems at the Bank for International Settlements in December 1997 or at the Bank of England in January 1998 or were invited to the Bank of England's Central Bank Governors' Symposium in June 1998.

[1] The Bank for International Settlements (BIS) publishes much detailed information about payment systems in the 11 Group of Ten countries (Belgium, Canada, France, Germany, Italy, Japan, Netherlands, Sweden, Switzerland, United Kingdom and United States), e.g., Bank for International Settlements (annual) and Bank for International Settlements (1993). Recently the BIS (1998) has published case studies on payment system issues in 19 transitional and developing countries. The International Monetary Fund (IMF) has also published some useful material on payment systems in transitional and developing countries, e.g., Johnson *et al.* (1998) and Summers (1994).

[2] We reproduce the questionnaire in Appendix 1 and the answers to some of the questions in Appendices 2–14.

Table 1.1. The Bank of England Group

Industrial	*Transitional*	*Developing*
Australia	Armenia	Bahrain
Austria	Belarus	Barbados
Belgium	Bulgaria	Bermuda
Canada	China	Botswana
Finland	Czech Republic	Brazil
France	Hungary	Colombia
Germany	Latvia	Cyprus
Greece	Poland	Eastern Caribbean
Hong Kong	Russia	Egypt
Iceland	Slovak Republic	Fiji
Italy	Slovenia	Guyana
Netherlands	Tanzania	Jordan
New Zealand	Vietnam	Kenya
Norway		Korea
Portugal		Kuwait
Singapore		Lebanon
Spain		Malawi
Sweden		Malaysia
Switzerland		Malta
United Kingdom		Mauritius
United States		Mexico
		Morocco
		Mozambique
		Namibia
		Nigeria
		Pakistan
		Peru
		Saudi Arabia
		South Africa
		Swaziland
		Tonga
		Turkey
		Uganda
		United Arab Emirates
		Zambia
		Zimbabwe

No two central banks in the world are identical. There is a wide range of functions carried out by central banks in different countries and each central bank undertakes a different set of activities from the full list. But there are clear common themes. Central banks are typically the monetary authority. They are usually involved in financial stability issues and, in various ways, in payment system matters.

This book describes the variety of ways in which central banks are involved in payment systems, and this introductory chapter seeks both to explain why central banks are involved and to provide some form of framework as an introduction to the analysis. It does so by describing the central banks' objectives and then looking at the range of risks that can arise in payment systems. It discusses some of the choices that are faced in payment system design and then moves on to describe the environment in which those choices are made. It outlines some of the choices that have been made by considering recent trends in payment and settlement systems and concludes by discussing the process by which central banks can try to achieve their objectives for payment systems.

1.1 Central Bank Objectives

Most central bank activities can be considered under the heading of monetary stability or financial stability. Indeed, the Bank of England finds this distinction sufficiently useful to have organised the institution on that basis, with the Bank's new constitution reinforcing this distinction by providing a separate Deputy Governor for each of these two aspects of the Bank's responsibilities. When the decision to organise the Bank in this way was taken, each of the activities had to be grouped into one part of the Bank or the other. The area that caused most difficulties in determining its location was that dealing with payment systems. And the reason for the difficulty lies in the fact that the objectives and interests of payment systems fall clearly under both the financial and monetary stability headings.

On the monetary stability side there is an obvious need for a mechanism to carry out monetary operations in support of monetary policy. Without an efficient payment system, it is extremely difficult to ensure that monetary policy is implemented effectively. In addition, both government and the public expect the payment infrastructure to work and expect central banks to be expert on these issues. Payment systems are a key part of the infrastructure supporting economic activity. Without an efficient method of exchanging payment, commercial activity would be severely constrained.

On the financial stability side the concern is that problems in individual financial institutions may well first be manifested in the payment system. The payment system can then transmit this instability from one institution to another. Good payment system design can contain these effects but bad payment system design can exacerbate them. So central banks have an interest in payment system design to reduce the risk of a domino effect, i.e., one bank failure causing other failures.

In emerging economies the issues of ensuring an efficient mechanism for supporting economic activity and enabling monetary policy operations to be carried out may be paramount. In more developed countries, however, the reliability of payment systems is typically taken for granted; the issues which dominate tend to be those of reducing risk, particularly in sophisticated financial markets. For this reason, the Bank of England decided to locate work on payment and settlement policy in the financial stability wing but with a clear instruction that policy makers in this area should work closely with colleagues on the operational side located in the monetary stability area.

Central banks' objectives for payment systems, under both the monetary and financial stability headings, may be summarised as reducing risk and promoting efficiency in payment systems. Risk reduction is paramount, but the promotion of efficiency is a complementary goal. Efficiency has many dimensions that broadly can be encapsulated by cost, speed and robustness. Robustness encompasses both the reliability of the service and the certainty of its effects, which may depend on the clarity of the rules or the precision of the relevant legal framework. It is perhaps obvious that efficiency is a desirable objective in its own right but, in addition, it may well be necessary to achieve the risk reduction objective. Typically, users have a choice about whether or not they use particular systems. There is no point developing a very safe system if nobody is prepared to use it. So the risk reduction and efficiency objectives have to be pursued in parallel but recognising that, while market participants may have an equal interest in the promotion of efficiency, they may not have as strong an interest in risk reduction if the private and social risks are different. As a result, it is sometimes left to the central bank to highlight the risk reduction questions.

1.2 Risks in Payment Systems

There are many different types of risk raised by payment systems including legal, operational, security and various forms of economic risk. Legal risks are one aspect of the need for certainty about how the system operates. Participants need to know what happens in different circumstances. If a participant defaults, for example, what will be the impact on other participants? This is particularly important where a payment mechanism is part of a settlement system, e.g., for settling securities. Good design of a securities settlement system involves the synchronised exchange of title to the security with final funds. This is the principle of delivery versus payment (DVP). But it is a satisfactory mechanism only if there is little doubt that title has in fact moved when the funds move (and vice versa).

Operational risk is perhaps more obvious. It is the risk of system malfunction because of information technology or mechanical failure, which may include problems in the wider infrastructure, such as an unreliable electricity supply or failures in the national communications infrastructure. It is extremely difficult to have a reliable and safe payment system without an adequate legal framework and basic social infrastructure.

Security risks are perhaps also relatively apparent. They arise from fraud or other abuse of the systems. Payment systems must be designed in a way that ensures that users or operators cannot interfere with the integrity of the data being transmitted or the instruments being exchanged. There need to be adequate safeguards and audit trails.

Economic risks come in many different forms but can be divided broadly into credit and liquidity risks. Credit risks generally arise as a consequence of the failure of a participant. One form of credit risk is market risk, also known as replacement cost risk, which is larger the greater the gap between a contractual agreement to make a payment and the settlement of that obligation. For example, if a participant has entered into a foreign exchange or securities transaction with a counterparty, and the counterparty fails before fulfilling its side of the bargain, the price of the asset may have moved against the seller. The difference in price is the market risk. An even more important credit risk (in the sense of involving larger values) faced in payment and settlement systems is principal risk. That is the risk of losing the entire value of the payment. It may arise in a payment system that is insecure or in a settlement system where the exchange of payment for a security (or other counter-value) is not synchronised, or in a system which does not have adequate loss-sharing arrangements.

Liquidity risks arise not only as a consequence of an insolvency but also as a result of any failed delivery. These may be caused by technical problems either with the party due to pay or with the system. Liquidity risks occur when a participant does not receive an expected payment but has obligations to make payments to other counterparties; these obligations may then be difficult to fulfil. In some cases, central banks may be the only realistic source of liquidity in the short term.

The way these risks arise in different systems depends very much on local circumstances, such as the type of economic activity as well as the payment instruments and the payment system(s) used in the particular country. For example, credit and debit transfer instruments produce somewhat different types of risks. But each country faces similar broad design choices in developing its payment systems.

1.3 Payment System Design

The case studies in this book look in more detail at some specific examples of design choices that have to be made. The choices will depend on many factors including the volumes in the system and their values (notably whether they support wholesale or retail activities), available technology and the development of the economy.

Two major areas of choice concern the means of processing or clearing the payments and the means of settling the resultant interbank obligations. Payment processing may be carried out in real time or on a batch basis where payment instructions are collected over a specific time period and then processed all at the same time. The key choice regarding interbank settlement is whether the basis of settlement should be gross or net. In a gross system obligations are settled one by one, whereas in a net system they are accumulated and offset. The net differences are settled periodically, typically at the end of the day. In addition to differences in the number of accounting entries that have to be made, there is also a legal distinction between gross and net settlement. Obligations in a gross system are legally settled individually, whereas net positions are the legally binding obligations in a net system. Real-time processing may be used in conjunction with either gross or net settlement within a payment system. Similarly, batch processing of payments may be more frequently associated with net settlement, but batched payments may also be legally settled individually.

A basic choice in payment system design is whether to adopt electronic means of clearing and settlement or to rely on paper processing. Electronic systems are usually preferable for high volume systems as they can be cheaper and avoid mistakes being introduced in the data after they are "captured" electronically. But paper systems can be more flexible. Further choices include whether a system should have centralised (e.g., at a clearing house) or decentralised processing of payment instruments, and whether the system should be nationwide in coverage. Typically, large-value systems are centralised and nationwide in scope, while some countries have found advantages in regional subsystems for retail systems. Finally, the designers of payment systems must decide whether the system operates on a credit transfer basis, where the payer initiates the transaction, or on a debit transfer basis where the payee initiates the transaction.

These choices are not always easy to make and no particular choice is likely to be right in all circumstances. Much depends on the characteristics of a particular economy and its payment flows, and these characteristics change over time.

1.4 The Environment

It may be worth recalling some familiar themes about how the financial economic environment is changing. The rate of technical progress is very rapid. Advances in information technology with ever more powerful and cheap microprocessor chips have encouraged the development of new ways of organising payment systems and, in particular, have increased the possibility of real-time payment processing. At the same time, the range of payments to be made and financial instruments to be settled has grown rapidly because of free capital movements and rapid growth in world trade. These trends have reinforced the globalisation of the industry; the size of firms participating in many payment activities has increased sharply.

Moreover the volumes and values being handled in payment systems across the world have grown rapidly (Crockett 1998, p. 3). The most dramatic examples are in the field of foreign exchange settlement where the total *daily* value of payments generated by foreign exchange activity amounts to some \$3 trillion (\$3,000,000,000,000). To put that figure in a comparative context, the value of payments through the United Kingdom's large-value transfer system is around £150 billion (\$250 billion) per day. This, in turn, implies that daily turnover in the United Kingdom's large-value payment system equals one-quarter of its gross domestic product (GDP).

While the numbers are getting bigger, there is greater complexity because of the increasing proportion of payment activity that is cross-border. This creates complicated payment chains and the possibility of conflicts between the laws of the jurisdictions involved or, at the least, some uncertainty about which of them would apply in different cases.

1.5 Payment and Settlement Trends

Against this background it is possible to see some patterns in the choices that have been made in different countries about the design of payment and settlement systems. On the *structural* side it is apparent that there is a general move towards greater use of real-time gross settlement systems for large-value payments. This trend is not universal—the largest payment system in the world is New York's Clearing House Interbank Payments System (CHIPS), which processes about 60 percent of the value of dollar payments. While CHIPS is currently a net system with end-of-day settlement, it has recently announced plans to evolve into a hybrid system with settlement of matched batches of payments throughout the day. From January 1999, the Euro Banking Association's (EBA) net end-of-day settlement system seems likely to obtain a relatively large share of payments in euros, the new European currency. But all the Group of Ten (G-10) countries and the countries of the European Union (EU), with the exception of Canada which has a large-value net settlement system possessing many of the characteristics of a real-time gross settlement (RTGS) system, have, or are developing, RTGS systems. Many other countries are also developing such systems. In Africa some of the smaller economies are cooperating in a joint development of an RTGS system. Throughout the world there is also a trend towards greater centralisation and fewer regional payment systems, particularly in the development of national large-value systems where there is a need to provide a payment infrastructure to support monetary policy implementation. This trend is also apparent in retail systems because of the increasing economies of scale in routine processing.

In small-value payment systems there is trend towards greater use of plastic. Plastic cards may take the form of credit cards, debit cards or electronic money (e-money). Credit cards were the first to be developed and are now commonplace throughout the world. But debit cards have recently grown rapidly. In the United Kingdom, for example, the volume of debit card transactions now exceeds that of credit card transactions. Even the value of debit card transactions may exceed that of credit card transactions within a few years. Debit cards substitute in particular for cheques, which are more cumbersome and relatively expensive to process (although costs have been contained by cheque truncation, which allows much of the processing to be carried out electronically). Electronic money, particularly in its network form, remains at the experimental stage in most countries although there have been some conspicuous successes with e-money cards, e.g., in Denmark. It seems very likely there will be rapid growth of electronic money cards, and perhaps network money, in the next few years as encryption methods improve and consumer acceptance increases.

The other structural trend in retail systems has been towards greater use of automated clearing houses, which provide electronic debit and credit mechanisms. In the United Kingdom, 70 percent of employees are now paid by direct credit transfer to their bank accounts and an increasing proportion of regular bills (for example to utility companies, local authorities, insurance companies and similar service providers) are paid by direct debits.

On the securities side there is a similar movement away from paper and towards electronic methods of settlement with increasing use of central securities depositories (CSDs). Such CSDs permit dematerialisation (the replacement of paper securities with electronic records) and may also provide arrangements for reducing risk in settlement, e.g., by providing a central counterparty and margining the exposures of participants. Moreover, securities settlement systems are improving their links to payment systems and developing improved forms of delivery versus payment.

On the *behavioural* side, there is probably greater awareness of risk issues in payment and settlement design. This is driven partly by central bank encouragement as, for example, in the case of foreign exchange settlement where central banks have been encouraging market participants to recognise the enormous risks involved. One of the features of this central bank campaign is to make banks and other market participants realise that reducing risk is not just a matter of good payment system design but also of good banking practice. For example, in the case of foreign exchange settlement a G-10 study on foreign exchange settlement risk showed the importance of reconciling funds received through correspondents in order to prevent potential exposures to individual counterparties accumulating (Bank for International Settlements 1996).

As in other industries, the payments industry is characterised by greater competition both between participants and between systems. There are fewer barriers to entry and greater opportunities for cross-border activities. This increased competition is particularly visible in Europe where payment systems that were relatively protected when operating only in domestic currencies will, from January 1999, all operate in euro and so be in direct competition with each other. This has focused greater attention on costs and pricing policy and has highlighted the importance of economies of scale in the business.

A further behavioural trend in payment and settlement systems has been increasing recognition of the need for liquidity management. This has become more important because of the development of real-time payment and settlement systems, shorter settlement cycles including more same-day markets, as well as developments such as DVP in securities markets and prospectively PVP (payment versus payment) in foreign exchange settlement. All these changes have increased demand for liquidity and reinforce the need for good management of liquidity in both funds and securities.

1.6 Managing Change

No central banker believes that existing payment and settlement structures, or the behaviour of market participants, are perfect. So all central bankers face the question of how to manage change in each particular payment and settlement system.

If central banks want to achieve change, they must decide how to do it. Typically, the central bank is directly involved, although there may well be other important agents involved in the process. In the United Kingdom, for example, the Association for Payment Clearing Services (APACS), the private sector association of commercial banks, is active in payment system development and cooperates in this closely with the Bank of England.

There are different ways of achieving change. It is possible to impose change in some ways and sometimes a statutory basis for the change can help. But while statutory action may enable a central bank to impose a particular structure, it may not enable a central bank to ensure that all participants behave as it would wish. In practice, whether central bankers adopt a statutory or nonstatutory approach, they must invariably achieve "buy in" from the participants of the payment system to the strategy that the central bank is trying to implement. This involves persuasion and influencing the opinion formers in the market in order to build a consensus in favour of the direction of change. If the market understands the central bank's objectives and shares its goal, participants are less likely to be suspicious of the changes needed to achieve them.

In the United Kingdom, the Bank of England had sought to achieve consensus on the changes required through a number of routes. First, the Bank publicises its views in regular bulletins, consultation papers and through public speeches. Second, the Bank also has regular direct contact with the main payment system participants, both individually and collectively through organisations such as APACS, the British Bankers' Association and other representative bodies. Third, the Bank keeps its strategy under regular review to ensure that its aims are set in a clear framework and with a realistic timetable for achievement. The Bank of England's own immediate objectives can be summarised under payment, securities and foreign exchange settlement systems.

On the payments side, the Bank of England has been very keen to adopt an RTGS system for large-value payments. The United Kingdom's large-value sterling system—the Clearing House Automated Payment System (CHAPS)—converted to RTGS in April 1996. The Bank of England is now working to ensure that the pan-European RTGS system for euro payments (TARGET) and the United Kingdom's connection to it—CHAPS euro—will be efficient and reliable.

On the securities settlement side, the Bank of England has published a report, following extensive consultation with market participants, that recommends amalgamating the United Kingdom's various securities settlement systems as necessary steps to improving their efficiency and achieving a full DVP mechanism in the United Kingdom.

Finally, as part of an internationally coordinated initiative, the Bank of England has been encouraging improvements in foreign exchange settlement methods, through changes by both individual banks and the industry as a whole, to reduce the massive exposures in the foreign exchange settlement process. The Bank believes that these objectives are now widely shared by the market. Nevertheless, there is still some way to go before they are all achieved.

1.7 Overview

Payment systems lie at the heart of all market economies because virtually all economic transactions require the use of a payment instrument.

Total resource costs of making payments typically absorb at least 3 percent of GDP in most economies (Hancock and Humphrey 1997, p. 1574). Chapter 2 examines the availability and use of alternative payment instruments. We illustrate the diversity of payment instruments and the intensity with which such instruments are used across the BoE group. We also examine the determinants of the demand for and supply of these alternative instruments.

Chapter 3 examines the development of payment systems and compares relevant features of alternative systems. Payment systems raise numerous issues—economic, legal, institutional, behavioural, managerial, etc. Here we start by sketching the development of payment systems and examining the relative importance of different types of payment risks during this development process. We then consider how payment system design affects payment risks. The chapter ends with some comments on the lengths of settlement cycles in the BoE group and a discussion of some development issues.

The efficiency of payment arrangements is important both directly in terms of resource costs and indirectly in terms of effects on other economic activities. Since the 1970s, there has been an increasing recognition of the risks associated with payments. So one analytical approach is to examine payment system risks in an adapted Markowitz-Tobin portfolio model. In this modification, there is a tradeoff between risk and cost along the efficiency frontier: risk reduction requires higher cost of payments. Chapter 4 uses this approach to set the stage for a more detailed theoretical analysis of the two major types of payment system used for large-value payments, RTGS and deferred net settlement (DNS) systems.

The recent adoption of RTGS systems in industrial, transitional and developing countries raises many interesting questions of design. Rather than attempting to cover a comprehensive range of issues here, we concentrate on two in Chapter 4: efficiency and liquidity provision. For any given set of payment orders, the liquidity needs are identical in RTGS and DNS systems. While the provision of liquidity in a DNS system is largely implicit, it is explicit in an RTGS system. Explicit liquidity demands are far higher for RTGS than DNS systems because, as a rough rule of thumb, $100 in gross payments can be settled by an end-of-day net transfer of $1. Offsetting flows in RTGS systems help reduce liquidity needs but an RTGS system might still require about 10 percent of the gross flows in terms of explicit liquidity provision.

But if central banks meet the significantly increased demands for intraday liquidity produced by the RTGS environment, can they prevent this injection of liquidity from precipitating monetary consequences by spilling over into overnight and longer maturity liquidity provision? In Chapter 5 we argue that such consequences can be prevented in all situations, but that clear policies must be promulgated to deter banks from incurring any risk that they might be unable to repay intraday credit to the central bank at the end of each day. This is particularly important in the context of a managed exchange rate.

Chapter 6 starts with the observation that failure in the payment system can produce a domino effect impinging on financial stability and monetary policy implementation. These and other externalities provide the main justification for intervention but raise the question: can the central bank perform better than the market when confronting a market failure? The central bank's objectives are to reduce risk and promote efficiency, whose components are speed, cost and reliability. Here we focus on the role of central banks in transitional and developing countries, using Poland as the main case study.

Payment systems are also important from the central bank's perspective in that they impinge in various ways on monetary policy and financial stability. Promoting sound and secure payment systems constitutes one of the Bank of England's core purposes because this activity promotes financial stability and facilitates implementation of monetary policy. So we then analyse the linkages between payment system policies, on the one hand, and monetary policy, exchange rate regimes and financial stability, on the other, in Chapter 7.

It should be clear from this introduction that the issues faced by individual countries differ. But equally there are some common themes and issues. All central bankers can learn from comparing experiences and discussing objectives, options and strategies. This is precisely the aim of the academic workshops and projects hosted by the Bank of England's Centre for Central Banking Studies. The origins of this book lie in the first such workshop held in January and the accompanying project that ended with a one-day conference in March 1998.

Chapter 2

Payment Instruments

2.1 Introduction

PAYMENT INSTRUMENTS COMPRISE CURRENCY, cheques, other debit transfer instructions, credit transfer instructions, credit and debit cards, and electronic money. Fragmentary estimates indicate that cash is still used in the majority of payment transactions (i.e., volume) in all countries,[1] but that these transactions tend to constitute a relatively small proportion of the value of total transactions (Borio and Van den Bergh 1993, pp. 9–10). For obvious reasons, however, these estimates of the volume and value of cash transactions are only indicative.

Comparing volumes is useful in that transaction costs are virtually unrelated to the value of any particular transaction, i.e., they are fixed costs. So the relative volumes of each payment instrument may relate to overall efficiency of a country's payment system. Value comparisons, in contrast, are particularly relevant for risk analysis because, *ceteris paribus*, larger values increase risk exposure.

2.2 Cash Transactions

Because no data exist on cash *flows*, we are obliged to use *stocks* of currency in circulation. One way of comparing cash transactions across the BoE group is to examine the stock of currency in circulation relative to GDP. This we do in Figure 2.1 by plotting ratios of GDP to currency

[1] Finland is close to or may have even crossed this half-way mark.

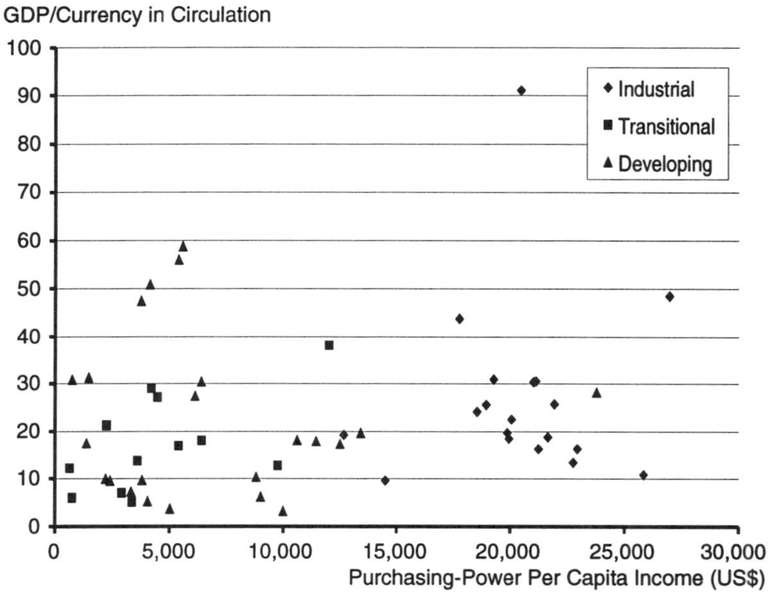

Figure 2.1. Gross Domestic Product/Currency and Per Capita Income

against per capita income, as measured using purchasing-power parity exchange rates to convert local currency values into dollars (*World Development Indicators 1997*, CD-ROM, Table 1.1). The GDP/currency ratios, i.e., income velocities of currency, tend to be lower in poorer countries than in richer countries. Given that this implies higher currency/GDP ratios in poorer countries, the explanation is presumably that cash tends to be more frequently used as the payment instrument in poorer than in richer countries.[2] As expected, income velocities of currency in circulation are positively related to inflation because inflation reflects the opportunity cost of holding currency (Stojanovic 1998, p. 3). So poor countries with high inflation exhibit velocities similar to those found in some rich countries with low inflation. Using analysis of variance and Kruskal-Wallis tests as well as regression analysis, Aleksandar Stojanovic (1998, pp. 3–5) finds that currency per capita and currency/GDP ratios are also affected across the BoE group negatively

[2]This relationship could also be explained by a higher proportion of economic activities taking place in the black economy where cash is used more intensively. This would also produce a greater underestimate of per capita income.

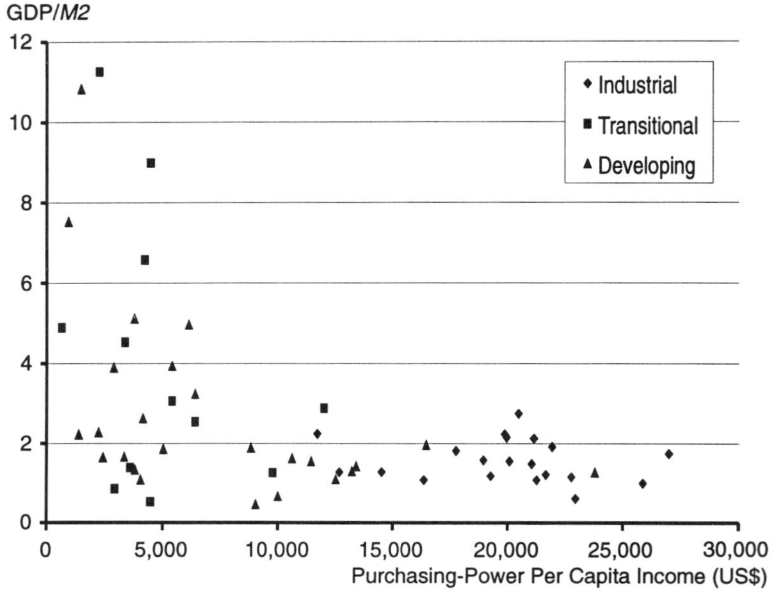

Figure 2.2. Income Velocities of M2 and Per Capita Income

and significantly by the maturity of the banking system, the level of development of the banking system, and the legal framework in which banks operate.

Figure 2.2 shows the relationship between income velocity of *broad money* (GDP/*M2*, where *M2* or broad money is defined as narrow money *M1* plus quasi-money *QM*, lines 34 plus 35 in *International Financial Statistics*, the data source used here) and per capita income. Evidently, the relationship in Figure 2.2 is the opposite to the relationship between income velocity of *currency* and per capita income in Figure 2.1. Income velocities of broad money are high in developing countries and low in rich countries, evidence that the income-elasticity of demand for *M2* exceeds one, i.e., *M2* is a luxury good. Again, income velocities of *M2* are positively related to inflation. In this case, therefore, poor countries with high inflation have considerably higher velocities than rich countries with low inflation.

2.3 Noncash Transactions

In contrast to cash transactions, noncash transactions are recorded and can be collated. Our first exercise with data on volumes and values of noncash transactions collected from our questionnaire responses is to examine the relationship between currency in circulation and volumes of noncash transactions. We would expect to find a negative relationship demonstrating that cash holdings fall as individuals and firms substitute noncash payment instruments for cash payments. David Humphrey, Lawrence Pulley and Jukka Vesala (1996, Table 1, p. 917) find a strong negative relationship between the value of currency holdings and the number of noncash transactions per person across 14 industrial countries.[3] This empirical finding provides some support for the use of the stock of currency as a proxy for the flow of currency-based transactions. Figure 2.3 illustrating this relationship for the BoE group confirms the relationship found by Humphrey, Pulley and Vesala (1996) for this much more diverse group of countries.[4]

Substantial foreign exchange business explains why the values of noncash transactions are so high in countries hosting international financial centres, such as Switzerland (109 times GDP), Japan (99) and Hong Kong (88), or providing reserve or vehicle currencies as well as an international financial centres, such as the United States (87 times GDP) and Germany (64) (Bank for International Settlements 1997*c*, Table 13, p. 43, Table 13, p. 62, Table 13, p. 87, and Table 13, p. 109; *International Financial Statistics*, CD-ROM, March 1998). In the Swiss Interbank Clearing (SIC), Switzerland's large-value transfer system (LVTS), about 90 percent of the value of transactions are foreign exchange-related. The comparable figures are 80 percent in the German Elektronische Abrechnung Frankfurt (EAF),[5] 50 percent in the United Kingdom's Clearing House Automated Payment System (CHAPS) and 50 percent in the United States' Clearing House Interbank Payments

[3]Because there are large holdings of deutsche marks and dollars outside Germany and the United States, Humphrey, Pulley and Vesala (1996, Table 1, p. 917) deflate the estimated per capita currency holdings by residents of these two countries by multiplying total currency in circulation by 0.65 and 0.40, respectively. We follow their procedure in constructing Figure 2.3.

[4]We suspect that numbers of noncash transactions are underestimated for countries that reported less than five noncash transactions per capita, so we removed these countries from this figure.

[5]From 1 January 1999, EAF stands for Euro Access Frankfurt.

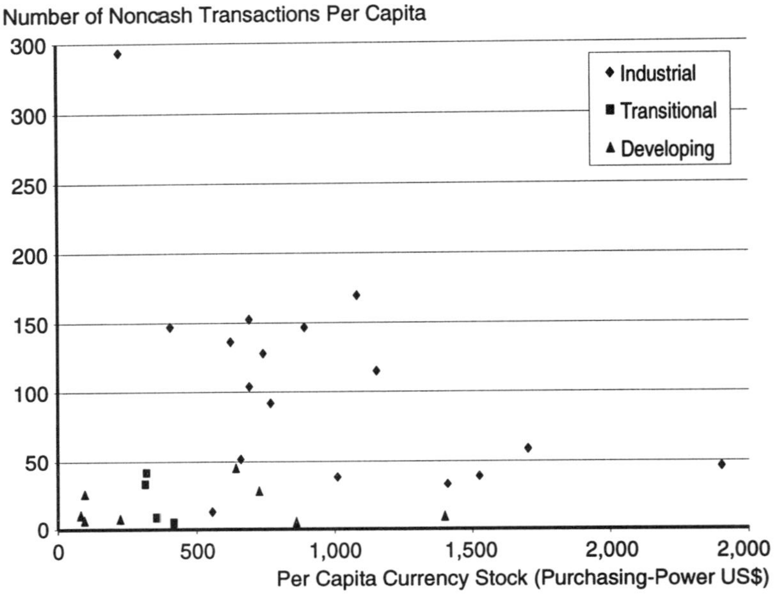

Figure 2.3. Per Capita Currency Stock and Noncash Transactions

System (CHIPS) (Bank for International Settlements 1996, p. 4). In the other G-10 countries, the ratio of transactions to GDP ranges from under 5 in Sweden to 43 in the United Kingdom (Bank for International Settlements 1997*c*, Table 13, p. 79, and Table 13, p. 96; *International Financial Statistics*, CD-ROM, March 1998). From the questionnaire response data, we estimate that ratios of transaction values to GDP in Guyana, Morocco and Tanzania are only 1.0, 1.2 and 1.6, respectively.

Figure 2.4 shows a clear relationship between the value of noncash transactions as a ratio of GDP and per capita income again measured by purchasing-power parity. In this respect, transitional economies do not differ from developing economies. Evidently, the value of transactions associated with one unit of GDP increases with per capita income, particularly for countries acting as international financial centres.

The value of transactions also rises in relation to GDP with higher inflation, in part because maturities of financial claims tend to be reduced as inflation accelerates. So the more frequent reinvestment of matured shorter-term financial assets, etc., increases transaction values without increasing GDP.

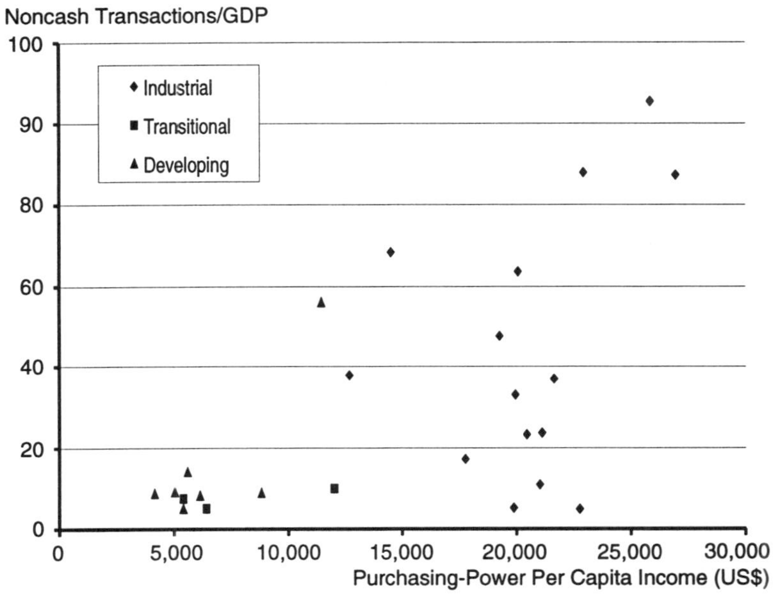

Figure 2.4. Noncash Transactions/Gross Domestic Product and Per Capita Income

Keith Bain and Peter Howells (1991) suggest that the value of transactions rather than income is the appropriate scale variable in a quantity theory-type demand for money function. This point is supported by the data in Figure 2.4, which reject the implicit assumption, that there is a stable ratio of transactions (by value) to GDP, on which many money demand analyses are based.

Were there a stable ratio of transaction values to money, i.e., a stable *transaction* velocity of money, the observed rising values of financial transactions in relation to income would be associated with declining *income* velocity, as has indeed occurred in several countries since the 1970s. More important, *fluctuating* values of financial transactions in relation to income would be associated with *volatile* income velocity. So information from the payment system may assist monetary policy making by improving money demand estimates.

Using data provided by the United Kingdom's Association for Payments Clearing Systems (APACS), Howells and Khaled Hussein (1997) find that the value of transactions is a better explanatory variable than GDP in a simple money demand ($M2$) function for the United Kingdom.

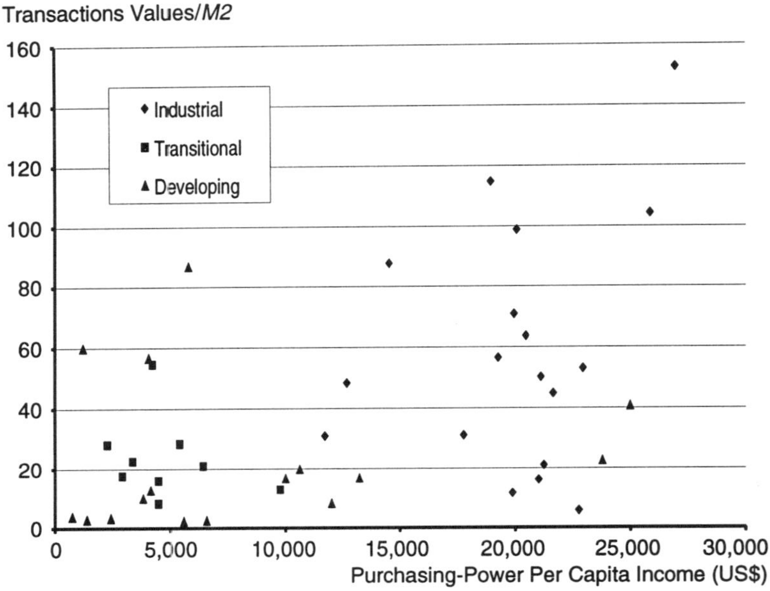

Figure 2.5. Transaction Velocities of M2 and Per Capita Income

They also show that the ratio of transactions to GDP in the United Kingdom increased erratically since the 1970s, first rising until 1974, then falling until 1976, then rising slowly until 1983. The ratio of transactions to GDP then accelerated rapidly from 1983 to 1988 before falling again until 1992. After rising somewhat from a local minimum in early 1992, this ratio appears to have been relatively stable only since 1993 (Howells and Khaled 1997, Figure 1, p. 373).

Figure 2.5 shows *transaction* velocities measured by dividing the value of noncash transactions by *M2*. In sharp contrast to the relationship between *income* velocities of *M2* and per capita income, higher incomes are associated in some, but not all, cases with higher transaction velocities in the BoE group; higher per capita incomes appear to be a necessary but not a sufficient condition for higher transaction velocities. One explanation is that there are more close substitutes for money in richer countries and so there are more opportunities for effective cash management. Financial innovation, such as the introduction of repurchase agreements, has gone hand in hand with a greater awareness of the possibilities for and potential of cash management techniques.

In 1970 values of noncash transactions nowhere exceeded 20 times GDP. Since then total values of noncash payments have risen dramatically due to a surge in financial activities (Borio and Van den Bergh 1993, pp. 5–6). In Germany, noncash transactions have increased from 9 times the value of GDP in 1988 to 64 times GDP in 1996 (Bank for International Settlements 1989, Table C, p. 19; 1997*c*, Table 13, p. 43; *International Financial Statistics*, CD-ROM, March 1998). In Japan, noncash transactions have increased from 18 times GDP in 1988 to 99 times GDP in 1996 (Bank for International Settlements 1989, Table C, p. 27; 1997*c*, Table 13, p. 62; *International Financial Statistics*, CD-ROM, March 1998). A considerable part of the recent rapid rise in the ratio of noncash transactions to GDP in countries such as Germany and Japan is due to rapid financial development as well as increased foreign exchange-related transactions over this period.

While we did not collect time-series data on noncash transactions from the BoE group, we can examine changes in currency holdings over time. Over the period 1986–1996, currency per capita increased in real terms by an average annual rate of 0.9 percent in industrial countries, it declined by 5.2 percent in transitional countries and also declined by 1.3 percent in developing countries.[6] Using pooled time-series data, Humphrey, Pulley and Vesala (1996, Table 2, p. 918) find that a 10 percent reduction in currency holdings is associated with a 6.8 percent rise in the number of noncash transactions per capita in their sample of 14 industrial countries. If the same elasticity applies across the BoE group, then the volume of transactions per capita would have increased annually by an average of 3.6 percent in transitional countries and by 0.9 percent annually in developing countries since 1986.

However, experience varied considerably across individual countries. In the industrial country group, real currency per capita increased at an average annual rate of 3.5 percent in Finland and declined at an average rate of 2 percent in Belgium. Real currency per capita declined at an average annual rate of 5.6 percent in Hungary and 4.9 percent in Poland. In the developing countries, real currency per capita increased by 7.8 percent annually in Korea and decreased by 14.3 percent annually in Peru.

[6] For the transitional countries, data for 1986 were available only for Hungary and Poland.

2.4 Noncash Payment Instruments

For the Group of Ten countries, the Bank for International Settlements (annual) reports both volumes and values of cheques issued, payments by debit and credit cards, paper-based credit transfers, paperless credit transfers, direct debits and others. Relative *volumes* are important because costs per transaction differ across payment instruments but hardly at all by value, i.e., it costs the same to process cheques for $1 and $100,000. From a policy viewpoint, volumes are important to the extent that private and social costs diverge. A zero marginal private cost of cheque use implies that the volume of cheques is too high from a social welfare viewpoint.

Cheques dominate as the main noncash instrument (by *value*) only in Canada, while in the other G-10 countries the lion's share of transactions (by value) takes the form of credit transfers, e.g., in 1996 credit transfers represented 95.7 percent of all noncash transfers by value in Germany, 99.8 percent in Switzerland, 94.4 percent in the United Kingdom and 87.7 percent in the United States (Bank for International Settlements 1997*c*, Table 9, p. 121). Because of incomplete questionnaire responses to the question about the composition of payment instruments, we have selected Italy as a representative industrial country, Hungary as a representative transitional economy and Malta as a representative developing country.

Using data obtained from our questionnaire responses for these three countries, Table 2.1 shows the distribution of noncash payments in these three countries. Paper-based instruments dominate in *volume* terms in both Italy and Malta, but electronic credit transfers constitute the dominant payment instrument both by volume and value in Hungary. By *value*, paper-based instruments dominate in Malta and constitute about 50 percent in Italy.

Among the industrial countries, Canada and the United States exhibit instrument choice that differs considerably from most others. In Canada, 41 percent by volume and 97 percent by value of noncash transactions use cheques; the figures are 75 percent by volume and 11 percent by value in the United States. These compare with 1.6 percent by volume and 0.1 percent by value in Switzerland (Bank for International Settlements 1997*c*, Table 8, p. 118, and Table 9, p. 120).

There is a noticeable difference in the composition of paper-based transactions between the transitional and developing country groups: credit transfers and cheques take equal share by volume in Italy, but cheques are used hardly at all in Hungary. In Malta, however, cheques

Table 2.1. Values of Noncash Transactions by Instrument Type in Representative Industrial, Transitional and Developing Countries (percent of total value)

Instrument	*Italy*	*Hungary*	*Malta*
		Volumes	
Paper-based instruments	63	1	57
Cheques	30	1	53
Paper credit transfers	33	0	4
Electronic credit transfers	10	57	3
Cards	9	43	40
Others	19	0	0
		Values	
Paper-based instruments	46	36	94
Cheques	18	0	74
Paper credit transfers	28	36	20
Electronic credit transfers	48	63	2
Cards	0	1	3
Others	7	0	0

dominate both in volume and value. By value, paper-based credit transfers represent 28 percent of noncash transactions in Italy, 36 percent in Hungary and 20 percent in Malta. Credit and debit cards are important for relatively small-value payments in both Hungary and Malta but represent minuscule percentages of total values.

Evidently and perhaps beneficially, the transition from a monobanking system has favoured credit transfer instruments in transitional economies. This follows naturally from the communist credit-directed system of resource allocation. After the monobank had credited an enterprise's account with its credit allocation, the enterprise then instructed the bank to make further credit transfers in payment for the resources acquired. This basic credit transfer instrument has been retained, in large part, during the transition in virtually all transitional economies.[7]

[7] Curiously, cheques have become popular in Poland. One of the disadvantages of such a debit instrument is illustrated by the cheque-kiting scam mentioned in section 6.5, p. 88.

Humphrey, Pulley and Vesala (1996, pp. 927–935) estimate the determinants of volumes of transactions made with alternative instruments in 14 industrial countries over the period 1987–1993. Given the difficulty of measuring the price attached to using alternative instruments, it is perhaps surprising that price elasticities, although estimated to be very low, were significant for paper giro, electronic giro and credit card instruments. Higher per capita incomes increase the volume of noncash transactions for all instruments except debit cards. Higher levels of violent crime increase the use of noncash payment instruments and greater banking concentration is associated with a lower use of paper-based payment instruments.

The determinants of payment instrument choice can be useful in predicting changes. For example, rising per capita income is associated with greater use of electronic payment instruments. This is relevant from the viewpoint of social welfare because marginal cost pricing is virtually nonexistent in the market for payment instruments. In many countries, the marginal cost to the user of cheques or credit cards is negative because of the benefit of float to the payer from the transaction date to the date when the account is debited.[8] For the United States, Humphrey and Allen Berger (1990, Table 2-1, p. 50) estimate that the social cost of a cheque payment was \$0.79 in 1987. However, the value of float to the payer resulted in a net private cost to the user of –\$0.04. Hence, cheque usage in the United States far exceeds the socially optimal level. The explanation for this distortion lies in part with subsidies provided by the Federal Reserve System and in part with an implicit subsidy in the form of nontaxation of banking benefits received in kind.

2.5 Welfare and Cost Considerations

In a number of the BoE countries, there is a perception that cash use is excessive. For the United States, however, Humphrey and Berger (1990, p. 51) argue that

[8]Float can be defined as the creation of windfall gains or costs to those involved in the payment process that arise when the accounting entries for the two sides of a payment are not posted simultaneously. So if A's account is debited *before* B's account is credited, the banks take an interest-free loan from B. Conversely, if A's account is debited *after* B's account is credited, B receives an interest-free loan from the banks. Float arises in several payment contexts; Chapter 4 examines more examples of float.

> The value of float associated with the use of cash is 1.18 times its real resource cost, while for checks it is 1.05. The important difference is that cash users *pay* this float transfer payment to the government, while check users *receive* it as a benefit from payees. In both cases, there is a substantial wedge between the private and social costs of a payment transaction with these two instruments. These wedges lead to market failure and encourage overuse of checks and underuse of cash.

What Humphrey and Berger fail to include in their private and social cost comparisons are costs of tax evasion and other crimes for which cash payments are used to provide anonymity.

In general, improving the efficiency of noncash payment instruments in terms of speed, cost and reliability is a more effective way of encouraging noncash transactions and discouraging cash transactions than attempts at prohibiting certain cash transactions. One reason why currency is preferred to noncash payment instruments in poorer countries probably lies in the considerably longer (and perhaps less reliable) clearing cycle in developing than in industrial countries (see Figure 3.3, p. 41).

Estimates for industrial countries show that paper-based payments are typically two or three times more costly than electronic payments (Humphrey, Keppler and Montes-Negret 1997, pp. 23–24). The slow conversion from paper-based debit instruments to electronic credit instruments can be explained, in large part, by the failure of the payments industry to charge users on a marginal cost pricing basis. Part of the explanation lies in the complexity of marginal cost pricing with a multifaceted product such as a bank account, but part of the explanation lies in distortions created by tax systems that tax interest but not services in kind. For this reason, both banks and their customers prefer implicit charging of cheque usage through low or zero deposit interest. In this way, customers are not taxed on the subsidised cheque-processing service and pay lower taxes on the lower or zero interest earnings on their deposit balances.

The challenge to central bankers lies in attempting to equate more closely social and private costs of using alternative payment instruments. Central banks in many industrial countries have already addressed distortions caused by central bank subsidies of payment facilities. Tax distortions have also declined to the extent that marginal tax rates have fallen. Nevertheless, habit and inertia may prolong overuse of previously subsidised payment instruments. So perhaps there is a legitimate role for central bank involvement to ensure that new socially cheaper electronic payment products meet minimum standards of reliability. Externalities from bad publicity provide at least one justification for such engagement.

2.6 Conclusion

While values of transactions using cash are impossible to measure with any accuracy, information from payment systems do provide data on the values of transactions using noncash payment instruments. Information on these *flow* values of noncash transactions may provide useful additional information for monetary policy purposes, because a stable relationship between transaction and income velocities of circulation evidently does *not* exist. So data on flow values of noncash transactions may assist monetary policy making by improving money demand estimates, where money is held, and hence a demand for money generated, partly for transactions purposes.

We find that choice of payment instrument is determined, in part, by a country's level of development. For example, cash appears to be used more frequently in poorer than in richer countries as evinced by the fact that GDP/currency ratios are lower in poorer than they are in richer countries. We detect substantial differences in choice of payment instrument across industrial, transitional and developing economies. Technological innovation and rising per capita incomes are associated with a shift from paper-based to electronic payment instruments. This change also corresponds to a shift from debit to credit instruments. Since paper-based payments are typically two or three times more costly than electronic payments, some central bank involvement to expedite the trend towards electronic transfers may be justified on welfare grounds.

Chapter 3

Payment Systems

3.1 Introduction

PAYMENT SYSTEMS RANGE FROM SIMPLE cash-dominated systems, as in the Seychelles, to systems involving a range of noncash payment instruments. The key feature of each payment system is the way payments are effected. In a currency-based payment system, payments are concluded by the transfer of currency notes from payer to payee; settlement takes place simultaneously with the transaction because currency represents final payment (currency constitutes "good funds", i.e., legal tender or central bank money) so no clearing function is needed. Because all other payment instruments involve at least one third party, the payment process is necessarily more complicated. Processing of cheques, for example, involves some means of clearing; settlement takes place through correspondent balances or by transferring balances of "good funds" in accounts held at the central bank. The same is true for all noncash payment instruments.

An important factor that influences the choice of payment system lies in the value of the transaction. The most efficient payment system in terms of the cost/risk tradeoff for transactions of $100 may well not be the same as it is for transactions of $1,000,000. So discussion of alternative payment systems often distinguishes between a large-value transfer system (LVTS) and a small-value transfer system (SVTS). Virtually all LVTSs settle through accounts held at the central bank. For this reason and because LVTSs play such a crucial role in economic affairs, central banks are invariably involved directly or indirectly in their operation. So, in the main, we concentrate on LVTSs rather than SVTSs in this chapter.

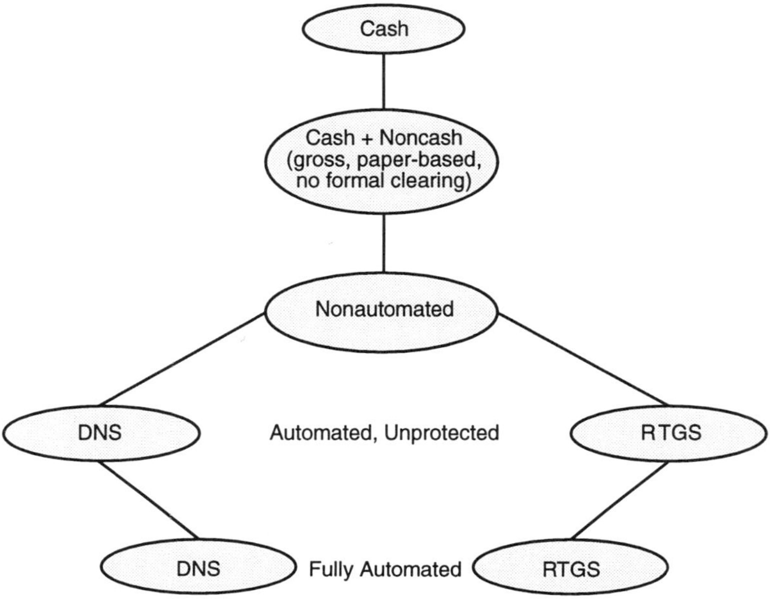

Figure 3.1. Development of Payment Systems

3.2 Stages of Payment System Development

Here we identify and analyse the following five stages of payment system development:

1. Cash;
2. Cash plus noncash instruments but with no formal clearing arrangements;
3. Nonautomated, unprotected DNS system;
4. Automated, unprotected DNS system with or without an RTGS system operating alongside it;
5. Fully automated and protected RTGS and/or DNS systems.

Naturally, further improvements after stage 5 will occur in the future.

Figure 3.1 provides a schematic illustration of this development sequence. Stage 1 is the primitive cash economy still encountered in rural areas of some developing countries where there are no banks. Transitional economies started their payment system development from stage 2, a cash circuit for consumers and a paper-based noncash circuit for enterprises in which all transactions were gross but with long lags between payment instruction and receipt of payment.

The prototype DNS system of stage 3 was a simple clearing house in London where banks exchanged cheques at the end of each business day. In this system, there were no credit limits between banks, in part because banks did not provide unconditional funds against deposited cheques. Such deposits became unconditional only after clearing and the confirmation that sufficient funds were available in the payer's account. In the case of credit transfers, however, the credit risk is more likely to fall on the receiving bank. With a credit transfer, customers and their receiving banks know that the payer had sufficient funds when making the transfer. So the receiving bank makes funds available to its clients and bears the risk that the payer's bank may fail in the interval between sending the credit transfer information and settling that payment in the end-of-day netting.

Most industrial countries had reached stage 4, predominantly with DNS systems, by the 1970s or 1980s. In such unprotected DNS systems, commercial banks provided free, unlimited, uncollateralised intraday credit. Until recently in unprotected RTGS systems, e.g., FedWire, the central bank provided free, unlimited and uncollateralised intraday credit. As risks in both net and gross systems were recognised, netting systems introduced caps and collateral (requirements that were subsequently incorporated into the Lamfalussy standards) and central banks required collateral or charged for intraday credit. With limited intraday liquidity, both DNS and RTGS systems have adopted prioritisation/queuing arrangements, while some DNS systems have increased the frequency of batch settlements during the day.

Automation increased speed and reduced costs, both driving and being driven by the dramatic increases in transaction values following both domestic and international financial liberalisation that took place in the industrial countries during these two decades. One consequence of the rapid increase in transaction values since the 1970s has been an increased awareness and recognition of payment risk. The traditional DNS systems of stages 3 and 4 involved unlimited implicit credit granted to the paying bank by the receiving bank from the time a payment instruction was received until the time of final settlement after clearing. For personal cheques, the risk is borne by the deposit-holder until the cheque is cleared and settled. But for cashiers' cheques and credit transfers, the risk is typically borne by the bank receiving the transfer instruction from the time the payment is credited to the customer's account until payment is received after clearing when the initiating bank has funds transferred from its central bank account to the receiving bank's account at the end of the day.

3.3 Risk Recognition and Protection in Payment Systems

It was the failure of Bankhaus Herstatt in 1974 that focused attention on payment risk in the context of cross-border transactions. The explosion in transaction values since then has magnified the extent of both domestic and cross-border settlement risks. So the Lamfalussy standards originally devised for cross-border and multi-currency netting and settlement schemes, as replicated in Table 3.1, have been commonly used to assess the robustness of domestic DNS LVTSs.

In addition, the increased use of credit as opposed to debit instruments has tended to transfer settlement risk from bank customers to the banks themselves. All large-value payment systems, such as New York's Clearing House Interbank Payments System (CHIPS), deal in credit instruments.[1] The typical netting arrangements for large-value payments enable recipients to transfer funds irrevocably and guaranteed by their bank on the basis of a receipt of funds before final settlement is achieved. In this way, the receiving bank is at risk to the sending bank rather than to the original payer (Bank of England 1994, p. 165).

In recognition of the increased intraday or daylight exposure to settlement risk, the London clearing banks joined the Bank of England in the late 1980s to study ways of reducing this risk. This culminated in a decision in 1992 to adopt an RTGS system. Increased intraday exposure to settlement risks and greater risk perception combined with reduced computing costs constitute the engines behind the recent and rapid worldwide adoption of RTGS.

By the 1990s collateral requirements, bilateral credit limits, debit caps and pricing had been introduced to protect most large-value transfer systems in industrial countries from payment risks. By the 1990s most of these large-value transfer systems were electronic. However, not all gross systems execute payment instructions in real time. Several transitional economies use deferred gross settlement systems.

[1] The exception is Canada's LVTS, which still handles large-value cheques.

Table 3.1. Lamfalussy Minimum Standards for Cross-Border Netting and Settlement Systems

Standard	Description
I	Netting schemes should have a well-founded legal basis under all relevant jurisdictions.
II	Netting scheme participants should have a clear understanding of the impact of the particular scheme on each of the financial risks affected by the netting process.
III	Multilateral netting systems should have clearly defined procedures for the management of credit risks and liquidity risks which specify the respective responsibilities of the netting provider and the participants; these procedures should also ensure that all parties have both the incentives and the capabilities to manage and contain each of the risks they bear and that limits are placed on the maximum level of credit exposure that can be produced by each participant.
IV	Multilateral netting systems should, at a minimum, be capable of ensuring the timely completion of daily settlements in the event of an inability to settle by the participant with the largest single net-debit position.
V	Multilateral netting systems should have objective and publicly disclosed criteria for admission, which permit fair and open access.
VI	All netting schemes should ensure the operational reliability of technical systems and the availability of back-up facilities capable of completing daily processing requirements.

Source: Bank for International Settlements (1990, p. 26)

Figure 3.1 draws the *protected* DNS and RTGS systems of stage 5 closer together than the *unprotected* systems of stage 4 because recognition of risk and the subsequent risk-reduction measures have produced some convergence between the two systems. For example, limited or costly intraday credit has led to batching or queuing in some gross systems, while risk recognition in DNS systems has exerted pressures to speed up the settlement cycle and, in some cases, to adopt more frequent net settlements. In some net systems, e.g., the Canadian large-value payment system, the central bank provides some explicit guarantee against systemic risk, while in a protected RTGS system commercial banks post collateral to cover the central bank's exposure. So payment risks are borne largely, but not necessarily exclusively, by the commercial banks in both protected DNS and RTGS systems.

In protected DNS systems, the typical loss-sharing arrangement ensures that posted collateral is sufficient to cover the failure of the institution with the largest possible amount owing to the system, i.e., the institution with the largest sender net debit cap. Typically, each participant sets bilateral limits on the implicit intraday credit it is prepared to extend to each other participant. A fraction α_1 of these bilateral limits constitutes that institution's own net debit cap, i.e., the maximum exposure that this sending institution can create in the system.

In the classical "survivors pay" scheme, each participant posts collateral equal to its largest credit line multiplied by a fraction α_2 ($\alpha_1 \leq \alpha_2$) calculated to ensure that the failure of the institution with the largest sender net debit cap is exactly covered by its own and all other participants' collateral.[2] Losses are shared on the basis of bilateral credit lines extended by the survivors to the failed institution. Since extending a larger credit line incurs a larger share in any loss, this encourages appropriate monitoring of all participants in the payment system. This is one of the major advantages of a "survivors pay" arrangement.

If a participant is denied sufficient credit lines to enable it to operate effectively, it may be permitted to post collateral against its own payments. In this case, full collateralisation of payments in excess of its sender net debit cap allows the participant to make payments exceeding the cap without jeopardising any of the other participants. With the central bank's agreement, this element of the payment arrangement becomes in most respects equivalent to RTGS. Such a collateral requirement is a "defaulter pays" arrangement in that a failed bank has already posted sufficient collateral to protect the surviving participants from loss. Its main defects are that it removes the incentive of participants to monitor each other and allocates more risk to unsecured creditors and depositors, which in turn may involve more risk for any deposit insurance agency. Exactly the same criticism applies to a protected RTGS system in which each bank posts collateral to cover its largest intraday credit from the central bank.

To persuade banks to extend sufficient credit to participants in its DNS system and to ensure same-day final settlement or same-day finality, the arrangements adopted by the Canadian Payments Association

[2]This meets the Lamfalussy minimum standard (Bank for International Settlements 1990). While these standards were designed primarily for cross-border transactions, they have been widely adopted as minimum standards for domestic net settlement systems.

involve the Bank of Canada insuring the payment system against a failure of more than one participant. This guarantee counteracts any reluctance of participants to extend intraday finality to their customers. With this guarantee, participants are assured that they will receive good funds at the end of the day under all circumstances. While there is some moral hazard created by this guarantee, it is greatly mitigated by the intramarginal collateral costs associated with any failure. In other words, the scheme resembles insurance against a very unlikely catastrophic event for which there is an extremely high deductible (Reain 1998, p. 4).

3.4 Choice of Payment System

Since 1980, the majority of industrial countries have adopted RTGS systems as the preferred system for large-value transfers. FedWire was the first RTGS system introduced in 1918; its modern version was developed in 1970. In the 1980s, the Netherlands (1985), Sweden (1986), Switzerland (1987), Germany (1987), Japan (1988) and Italy (1989) introduced RTGS systems. Since 1990, a substantial number of industrial, transitional and developing countries have adopted RTGS systems. All EU countries will have developed euro RTGS systems linked to the EU-wide RTGS system (TARGET) by the time it starts on 4 January 1999.

The BoE group exhibits a multiplicity of payment systems in use at present. Four main groupings can be identified: countries with only RTGS, countries with only DNS, countries with both RTGS and DNS, and countries with other types of payment systems. In countries with both RTGS and DNS systems, three subcategories appear: RTGS for high value transactions and DNS systems for retail arrangements, RTGS and DNS systems both used for wholesale and retail payments, and an arrangement with two RTGS systems, where one is restricted and the other is open, operating alongside net settlement systems. In the group that has other types, the most common is gross systems with deferred batched settlements usually at the end of the day or next day, although occasionally at set times during the day.

Another interesting aspect is that most of the respondent countries indicated that they are examining the possibility of adopting an RTGS system, mainly for large-value interbank settlement transactions. Net settlement together with other types of settlement systems are increas-

Table 3.2. Payment Systems in the Bank of England Group (percent of countries in each group)

Type	*Industrial*	*Transitional*	*Developing*
RTGS	86	46	25
DNS	86	62	83
Other	5	38	22

ingly used for retail transactions.[3] With such diversity of system design, risk strategies are equally diversified.

Table 3.2 shows that, within the BoE group, 86 percent of the industrial countries, 46 percent of transitional countries and 25 percent of developing economies in the BoE group possess RTGS systems.[4] The more rapid development of RTGS in transitional than in developing economies may seem surprising. However, it is a logical development from the deferred gross systems that transitional economies typically possessed in the 1980s. However, part of the explanation lies in the worldwide reduction in telecommunication and computing costs. The geographical size of a country may also provide another part of the explanation in that the advantages of electronic over paper-based payment instruments are relatively greater for large countries such as China and Russia than for small countries.

Preference for RTGS in transitional and developing countries is also due in part to the legal complexity of netting arrangements. Benefits of netting are greatly enhanced if net rather than gross obligations form the basis of bankruptcy proceedings. In this case, liquidators can claim only the failed institution's *net* obligations *vis-à-vis* individual counterparties or, in a clearing house context, *vis-à-vis* all clearing house members. Legally enforceable multilateral netting reduces the credit risk exposure of clearing house participants as a whole at the expense of increasing the credit risk exposure of other nonclearing house creditors.[5] It produces

[3]Large international banks have established card networks in the Czech Republic, Hungary, Korea and Saudi Arabia that service retail transactions in a variety of settlement schemes.

[4]Unfortunately, we were unable to distinguish between LVTSs and SVTSs for this table. Most DNS systems in the industrial countries are SVTSs.

[5]In the absence of legally enforceable netting arrangements, liquidators could and would collect all payments owed to the failed institution before considering claims for amounts

a moral hazard in that risk is pooled and requires complex legal provision that may be challenged, particularly for cross-border transactions (Flannery 1996, p. 810).

All G-10 countries possess at least one LVTS providing same-day final settlement. In Canada, this is provided by a DNS system, but in all other G-10 countries it is provided by an RTGS system. In the United States, both DNS (CHIPS) and RTGS (FedWire) systems provide same-day finality. Germany, France and Spain have also developed two same-day LVTS systems: DNS and RTGS systems in France and Spain. Germany has introduced its EAF hybrid batched settlement system alongside an RTGS system.

3.5 Risks at Different Stages of Payment System Development

All payment systems change over time. Systems develop from simple cash transactions to complex systems as new technologies and new ideas are incorporated. Volumes and values of transactions increase as economies grow and become richer and more monetised. The degree of risk exposure in payment and settlement transactions increases as volumes and values of transactions increase. Lengths of settlement cycles are reduced or even eliminated with the adoption of RTGS systems. As these changes are linked to the risks described in Chapter 1, specific stages of payment system development can be associated with particular payment system risk characteristics.

During the cash stage, settlement, credit and liquidity risks are nonexistent. There is some operational risk, but it is hardly significant. The main risk concerns security—principally the risk of theft of bearer instruments (bank notes), but also the risk of counterfeit. In the second stage, noncash instruments are used alongside cash, but without formalised clearing or netting arrangements. Clearing and settlement of these instruments are achieved therefore either on a purely bilateral basis between pairs of banks or via the central bank on a deferred gross basis. In this stage credit risks start to emerge if banks provide value against

---

owed. If bank *A* owed bank *B* $100 and bank *B* owed bank *A* $100 through their clearing house, failure of bank *A* before settlement would have no financial implications for bank *B* provided a legally enforceable netting arrangement existed. Without this legal provision, bank *B* would have to pay $100 to bank *A*'s liquidators and the $100 owed would be included in the total amount bank *A* owed to all other unsecured creditors.

debit instruments before the instruments are settled. Central banks may also incur risks if commercial banks do not possess sufficient funds to cover their gross obligations. Security risk declines but still remains relatively high. Operational risks become more noticeable. Because documents are processed manually and are physically transported, human error increases.

At the third stage (nonautomated and unprotected DNS), credit risks and liquidity risks become fully established with multilateral net settlement introducing systemic risk. At the same time, legal complications are introduced, particularly by netting arrangements and their relationship with legal provisions for insolvency. The relative importance of security risk further declines. At this stage the system may be operating with a few computers but is not fully automated.[6] Some additional increase in operational risk can therefore be anticipated.

In the fourth stage with a fully automated but unprotected DNS system (and perhaps with an unprotected RTGS system provided by the central bank), economic risk reaches its peak. If the legal basis of the payment system has not been clarified, legal risk too will rise. Given automation, security should improve further; automation should also reduce clerical error. Whether operational risk rises, falls or remains unchanged depends on contingency and backup facilities that are included in the automated system.

Finally in the fifth stage of fully protected DNS and RTGS systems, or hybrids of the two, the relative importance of the various sources of risk tend to equalise. Per unit of payment, overall payment risk falls dramatically. Whether or not it falls absolutely depends on how dramatic the accompanying increase in the value of transactions is. In any case, the end result is a very small risk of a very large catastrophe.

Figure 3.2 illustrates the relative importance of operational, legal, economic and security risks at these five stages of payment system development. In our view, legal risk increases monotonically, as does operational risk except perhaps in stage 4. Security risk tends to decline throughout the development process, at least until stage 5 when efforts have been taken to protect payment systems against operational and, particularly, economic risk. Economic risk rises dramatically until stage 5 when this risk is addressed most effectively in terms of caps, limits and collateral requirements.

---

[6]Many developing economies experience the first three stages at the same time. In Tanzania, for example, the three stages can be identified at district, regional and zonal levels.

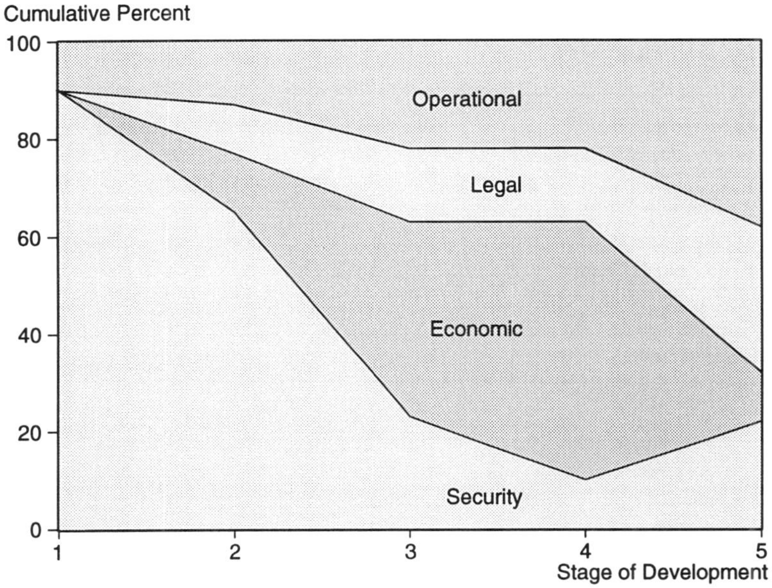

Figure 3.2. Relative Importance of Risks at Difference Stages of Payment System Development

In our questionnaire, we asked respondents to indicate what measures had been introduced to confront settlement risk in their various payment systems. Table 3.3 presents results across the three country groups. All countries protect their RTGS systems in one way or another. Most industrial country central banks provide unlimited intraday credit against collateral. In the majority of transitional and developing countries, the protection usually takes the form of limited (frequently zero) intraday credit from the central bank. Where central banks provide limited intraday credit, they invariably do so against collateral. However, some transitional countries provide limited intraday credit for payment purposes without collateral.

The questionnaire responses on risk protection measures in DNS systems indicate that, despite the fact that DNS systems are inherently riskier than RTGS systems, the majority of DNS systems in the BoE group are not protected against payment risk by intraday limits, collateral or loss-sharing arrangements, quite possibly because they are mainly retail payment systems. The transitional countries show the least use of collateral as a risk-protection device. This may reflect legal difficulties

Table 3.3. Risk Protection in Main Payment Systems (percent of countries in each group)

Type of Protection	*Industrial*	*Transitional*	*Developing*
	Real-Time Gross Settlement Systems		
Credit limits	17	100	78
No intraday credit	6	67	45
Limited intraday credit	11	33	33
Collateralised credit	89	17	56
Unprotected	0	0	0
	Deferred Net Settlement Systems		
Intraday limits	17	44	13
Collateral	28	0	50
Loss-sharing	28	0	10
Unprotected	56	56	50

involved in pledging collateral, a shortage of suitable financial assets to post as collateral, and inadequate collateral transfer mechanisms (i.e., in the securities settlement system).

3.6 Major Factors Affecting Payment Systems Risks: The Design

If payment system risks are to be minimised, the forces that cause such risks must be understood. A payment system will provide unsatisfactory risk protection if it is deficient in security, reliability, timeliness, certainty of value and accuracy. These measures of the robustness of a payment system are tested when values and volumes of payment transactions increase, but also when payment lags (settlement periods) are long. The deficiency of the system may also be a result of inappropriate design. Hence, the volume of transactions per period, the value of transactions per period, the average transaction value, the length of the payment cycles and the payment system design constitute the main factors influencing the gravity of risks in payment and settlement transactions. This section examines these factors as they manifest themselves in developing and transitional economies.

The first encounter with the major factors influencing payment system risks is during the development stages of payment and settlement systems, and particularly during the design phase. An appropriate design presents the greatest challenge to the developers and modernisers of national payment systems. A payment system should be designed to enhance security, reliability, certainty of value, accuracy and timeliness. The design must take into account the values and volumes of transactions that will be involved as well as projected settlement lags.[7] At the same time, an appropriate design must accord with the existing business and economic environment.

Three elements often appear crucial:

- inadequacy of data regarding existing payment arrangements;
- technological weaknesses;
- the ever-changing complexities of payment and settlement systems.

A number of developing and transitional economies are now developing their payment systems, while the industrialised nations are improving their existing systems.[8] All would like to have a system that is risk-free or at least a system that is resilient to the most ubiquitous payment system problems. The developing economies wish to learn from the experiences of those countries that are ahead in the field and, if possible, to adopt their systems. However, they have learnt quickly that their environments are very different from conditions in the countries possessing the systems they would like to adopt. At the same time, globalisation of payment transactions increases the pressure to accept technological change and to adopt sophisticated payment systems.

Two major and related questions are: (a) Do the developing countries have any choice? and (b) Can they afford these sophisticated arrangements? The answers are not straightforward. As already argued, the developing economies need to adopt a payment system that is robust and modern sophisticated systems provide state-of-the-art solutions to this need. At the same time, the developing countries are participants in

---

[7] Peter Allsopp (1995) argues that, in addressing the issues of value of transactions, volume of transactions and reduction of settlement lags (to zero), an RTGS design has many benefits.

[8] See Israel Sendrovic (1995) for an excellent explanation of the technological changes that are taking place in FedWire.

international trade and so have settlement arrangements with industrialised economies. They must therefore adopt minimum levels of technological development in payment systems simply to communicate with their correspondents. In that respect their choices are indeed limited.

The most commonly known designs of payment and settlement systems are the RTGS and DNS systems. In the process of addressing payment system risk issues and initiating remedial measures, industrialised nations have developed many versions of these two payment system designs to the point where these two systems are converging. Many varieties of net settlement systems as well as of gross settlement systems are now in use.[9] One of the complications being faced by developing economies in selecting a suitable design for their systems is the multiplicity of varieties available under different environments. And, most important, payment and settlement system designs are constantly changing and becoming increasingly complex.

3.7 Length of Settlement Cycles

Payment and settlement exposures can exist from the time the payment instructions are given until the time the payment is settled with finality at the account of the payee's bank.[10] The longer the settlement cycle, the longer the period of exposure.

Figure 3.3 showing the average length of settlement cycles in days illustrates the fact that cycles are longer and so risks are greater in poorer countries than they are in richer ones. Using both parametric and nonparametric tests, Aleksandar Stojanovic (1998, pp. 6–8) finds significant differences in lengths of settlement cycles between industrial, transitional and developing countries. His regression analysis indicates that the average length of settlement cycles are negatively and significantly affected by per capita income and inflation.

As an example, the survey results indicate that Tanzania posts one of the longest (and most variable) settlement cycles of between three

[9] The SIC system with its three to four hours' delays due to the queuing system is hardly a real-time settlement arrangement, while same-day finality in the Canadian net settlement system facilitated by central bank underwriting makes this system similar to an RTGS system.

[10] In foreign exchange settlement, the exposure is the full amount of the currency purchased and exists from the time a payment instruction for the currency sold can no longer be cancelled unilaterally until the time when the currency purchased is received with finality (Bank for International Settlements 1996).

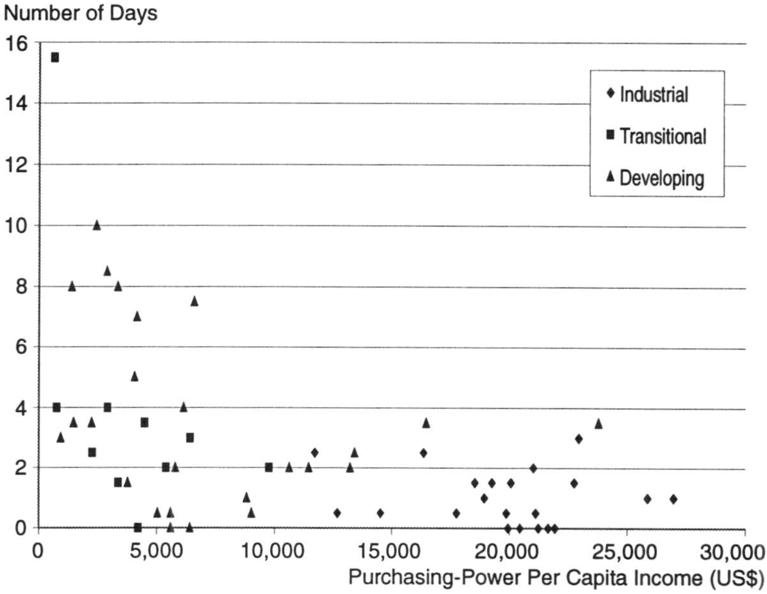

Figure 3.3. Average Length of Settlement Cycles and Per Capita Income

and twenty-eight days. On the basis of Tanzania's transaction values for 1996, even a three-day cycle implies a value of unsettled payments of about TZS40 billion, while a cycle of twenty-eight days implies a value of over TZS350 billion. These are large amounts at risk by any standard.[11]

While many attempts have been made to reduce the lengths of payment cycles, such attempts will not produce lasting benefits in terms of reduced risk and increased efficiency if such shorter cycles remain subject to large or even larger variability. A certain five-day cycle may be preferable to an unpredictable three-day cycle that ranges from one to five days or even longer.[12]

[11]The exchange rate in 1996 fluctuated around TZS600 to $1. In dollar terms, therefore, these values are approximately $65 million and $610 million, respectively.

[12]Theo Lubke (1998) explains how shortening the settlement cycle for United States' corporate and municipal securities to reduce credit risk exacerbated operational risks.

Table 3.4. Obstacles to Payment System Development

Type	*Industrial*	*Transitional*	*Developing*
Legal framework			
Poor	10	18	35
Satisfactory	60	27	35
To be improved	30	55	30
Technical infrastructure			
Poor	5	8	32
Satisfactory	90	38	42
To be improved	5	54	26
Maturity of the banking system			
Poor	0	17	16
Satisfactory	95	0	40
To be improved	5	83	44

3.8 Some Development Issues

Many central banks have been actively engaged in the development of their countries' payment systems. In our questionnaire, we asked all central banks to describe the main obstacles faced in this process. Table 3.4 summarises the results by broad categories.

We also asked about the central bank's strategy towards payment system reform and development and the extent to which commercial banks were involved in planning such strategies. Table 3.5 provides the results of this question. Not surprisingly, we find a strong preference on the part of central bankers for evolutionary rather than revolutionary development of their countries' payment systems.

Convergence of payment systems, which appears to be taking place across the world, springs from three basic causes. The first is the worldwide adoption of RTGS systems for large-value payments. This global adoption of RTGS systems has occurred because of (a) cost reductions in computing and telecommunications; (b) greater risk recognition; and (c) simpler legal infrastructure requirements for RTGS compared with DNS systems. The second cause of global convergence is the increasing similarity between RTGS and DNS systems for large-value payments. The third is increased global competition (Folkerts-Landau 1997). Perhaps

Table 3.5. Payment System Strategy and Commercial Bank Involvement

Strategy	*Industrial*	*Transitional*	*Developing*
Evolutionary	52	62	69
Leapfrogging	19	23	19
Not applicable	29	15	12

this third cause is the one that should be of most concern to central bankers because this competitive drive to reduce cost has the potential for increasing risk on a worldwide basis.

3.9 Conclusion

The relative importance of different types of risks to payment systems depends on their stage of development. Since most developing and transitional economies possess payment systems that approximate the earlier stages of payment system development in the industrial countries, the relative importance of payment system risks tends to vary across these country groups. However, the recognition of payment system risk has been universal. This suggests that most developing and transitional economies can leapfrog from stage 3 to stage 5 of payment system development, since risk protection, except protection against operational risk, is not dependent on expensive new technology.

Our main interest in this chapter has been how systemic risk in payment systems, especially in its current international dimensions, can affect developing and emerging economies. Much literature exists on various aspects of systemic risk; various methods for preventing it have been devised and introduced in both RTGS and DNS systems. In the United States, CHIPS is currently covered by sophisticated arrangements that address payment system risks in a DNS system. For minimising systemic risks in an RTGS system, the approach developed within the European Union and coordinated by the European Monetary Institute/European Central Bank (EMI/ECB) in the context of creating the pan-European TARGET system provides an excellent example. Many of these measures can be adapted without inordinate difficulty or expense to the specific conditions of most developing and transitional economies. Indeed, many developing countries have already taken such steps. Others delay doing so at their own peril.

Chapter 4

Deferred Net Settlement versus Real-Term Gross Settlement for Large-Value Transfer Systems

4.1 Introduction

IN THE MID-1970s, Boris Pesek (1976, p. 863) stated that demand deposit turnover was so amazingly fast in the United States as to make inescapable the conclusion that demand deposit balances were being operated at or close to *peak efficiency*. Therefore, Pesek concluded that demand deposits must constitute solely transactions, rather than precautionary or speculative, balances.

Pesek illustrated this improved "efficiency" by noting that transactions velocity in the United States had increased from 40 in 1964 to 105 in 1974. The 1974 figure, he claimed, represented the "technical limits upon the speed of turnover of deposits" (Pesek 1976, p. 863). Nonetheless, transactions velocity in the United States exceeded 500 in 1996, implying that demand deposits turned over on average twice on every working day of the year.[1]

In fact, velocity cannot be equated with efficiency. As is well known, velocity rises to extremely high levels during hyperinflations. But having to spend the morning's earnings during one's lunch break and afternoon's earnings on the way home hardly represents an efficient

[1] In the United States, the average daily turnover of bank reserve balances with Federal Reserve Banks has also risen—from 1 in 1960 to 30 in 1985 to over 60 in 1992 (Blommestein and Summers 1994, p. 26).

payment system. It is simply a consequence of the extraordinarily high opportunity cost of holding money.

As inflation accelerates deposits fail to increase in step with nominal GDP because households and firms choose to hold smaller money balances in relation to their expenditures because of the rising cost of holding money.[2] In contrast, bank operating costs tend to rise at least as fast as GDP. Hence operating costs as a percent of earning assets held by the banking system increase. For example, between 1977 and 1980 the real *M2* money stock in Turkey declined by 25 percent. Over the same period, however, the number of bank branches increased by more than 15 percent and the number of bank employees rose by over 10 percent. As Brazil's inflation rose from 13 percent to 41 percent, bank operating costs as a percentage of bank loans increased from 6 percent in 1952 to 24 percent in 1966. In fact, there is a tendency for operating costs to rise in real terms as inflation accelerates. In Argentina during the 1980s, accelerating and volatile inflation increased liquidity preference. Practically no deposits with maturities of over 30 days were held by 1985 (Fry 1995, p. 327). A week is a long time in finance under such volatile conditions, but rolling over deposits and loans on a weekly basis makes the system very costly.

4.2 An Analytical Framework

Given the diversity in payment instruments and systems discussed in Chapters 2 and 3, is there any analytical framework that can be applied to all countries and to all payment systems? Perhaps one can detect two universal characteristics of payment systems. To do this, we start with some simple history:

- Payment preceded money: barter.
- Credit preceded money: barter credit.

In a small, static, traditional society, e.g., Europe in the Middle Ages or a Pacific Island before the arrival of Captain Cook, there would be

[2] Even a competitive banking system cannot raise deposit rates of interest in step with inflation when it is subject to noninterest-earning reserve requirements. The reserve requirement tax burden, which increases with inflation, is passed on to depositors or lenders through lower inflation-adjusted/real deposit rates or higher real loan rates of interest.

no demand for a means of payment. All transactions could easily be arranged by barter exchanges or credit barter. In such a world of virtual certainty, everyone would know where to send his or her products and when and where to collect the goods and services provided in exchange.

Following Charles Goodhart (1989, Ch. 2), we suggest that uncertainty and transaction costs constitute the two prerequisites for a demand for money as a means of payment:

- Uncertainty produces a preference for immediate rather than postponed payment.
- Transaction costs produce a preference for payment in something that is generally acceptable as a means of payment. A chain of exchanges is more costly.

Uncertainty or risk, on the one hand, and transaction costs, on the other, are still the two main considerations for payment system analysis today. This is recognised in the analytical framework presented by Allen Berger, Diana Hancock and Jeffrey Marquardt (1996). This framework adapts the standard risk-return analysis used in finance by substituting cost for return: on the efficiency frontier, lower risk in a payment system can be obtained only at a higher cost. Figure 4.1 shows the efficiency frontier *FF* plotting combinations of risk and cost attached to the most efficient payment systems.[3] Efficiency is measured from a social welfare viewpoint incorporating all costs of payers and payees, as well as externalities. In other words, efficient payment systems cannot reduce risk without raising cost or reduce cost without increasing risk. Many factors, e.g., technological, institutional and legal, determine the position and movement of the efficiency frontier. Over time, innovations in these factors may shift the efficiency frontier towards the origin, so enabling reductions in both cost and risk.

To determine the optimal payment system, Figure 4.1 must incorporate a social indifference curve. Society would prefer less cost and less risk, but would be indifferent between various combinations involving lower risk and higher cost. The curve *II* connects points of indifference, i.e., there is no preference to be located at any particular point on the curve. This curve is the social indifference curve, implying that society

[3] An alternative but less intuitive representation would place a bundle of payment attributes on the horizontal axis replacing return in the standard risk-return tradeoff diagram. Of course, a bundle of "goods" in contrast to the "bad" cost attribute used here would tilt both the efficiency frontier and the indifference curve clockwise by 90°.

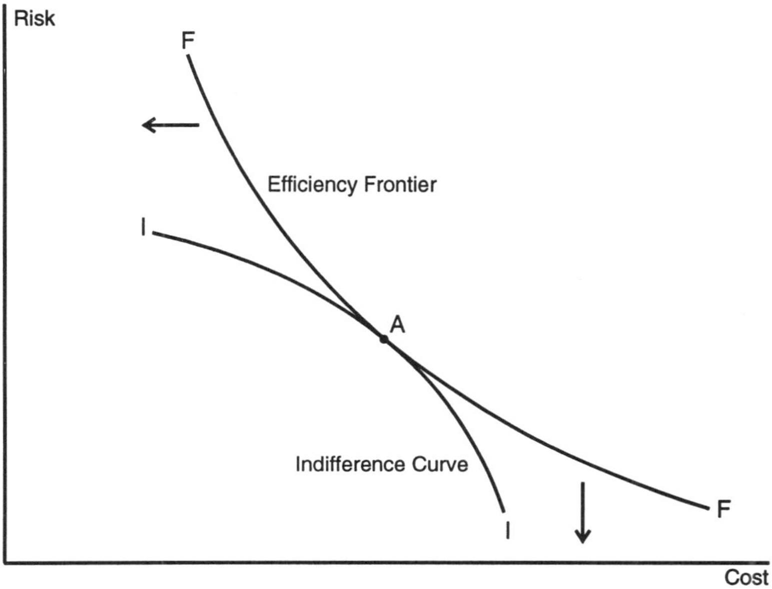

Figure 4.1. Risk–Cost Tradeoff along the Efficiency Frontier

as a whole holds a view on its preference or tradeoff between risk and cost.

When risk is high, society may be prepared to pay more per unit of risk reduction than when risk is low. In such case, the social indifference curve will be convex to the origin. Here the curve *II* indicates that at relatively high risks society is prepared to incur a relatively large cost for risk reduction, so the slope of the curve is relatively flat. But where risk is already low towards the bottom righthand side of Figure 4.1, society is prepared to incur only a small cost for further risk reduction. Indifference curves nearer the origin offer greater social welfare than indifference curves further away from the origin. So welfare is maximised at the point of tangency between an indifference curve and the efficiency frontier: it is not possible to move to a better indifference curve from point *A* in Figure 4.1

As with any two-dimensional representation of a complex system, Figure 4.1 omits several other crucial factors that determine the position of the efficiency frontier in risk–cost space. For example, monetary policy techniques may affect the position of the efficiency frontier. Figure 4.2 depicts this in a three-dimensional diagram as a rising plane

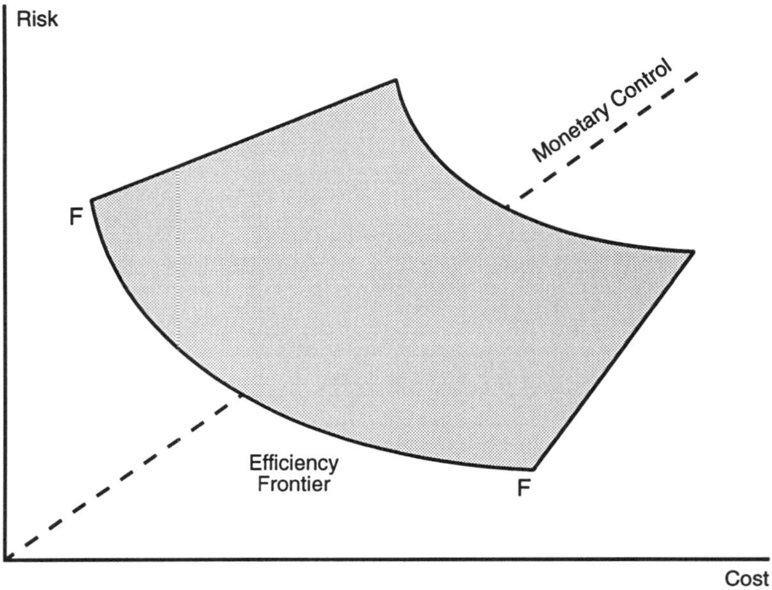

Figure 4.2. Risk, Cost and Monetary Control Tradeoffs along the Efficiency Frontier

such that greater monetary control can be obtained only at the expense of a less favourable risk–cost tradeoff in the payment system; this tradeoff is examined at some length in section 4.3. But indifference must now also be represented as a plane in which society trades off risk, cost and monetary control or price stability.

In reality, risk takes a variety of forms with economic, legal, operational and security risks constituting the main categories. Efficiency too combines speed, reliability and cost. Evidently, therefore, the problem of payment system choice and design is a multifaceted one with tradeoffs possible along a multiplicity of axes.

4.3 Deferred Net Settlement versus Real-Time Gross Settlement

One of the fundamental distinctions between LVTSs is that between RTGS and DNS systems. In the 1970s, payment systems in most industrial countries could be characterised as unprotected DNS systems. At that time, the United States was the only country to possess an RTGS system.

Both DNS and RTGS systems were unprotected in that payment risks, i.e., the risks of various kinds that payments would fail to be made, were ignored. In the DNS system, banks provided unlimited (and often unknown), implicit and unsecured credit from receipt of payment until net settlement after clearing at the end of day or beginning of the next day. In the United States, the Federal Reserve System provided unlimited, free and unsecured intraday credit to all users of FedWire. So, in theory, payment risk is borne by the commercial banks in a DNS system but by the central bank in an unprotected RTGS system. In practice, however, failure in a DNS system may be so calamitous that the central bank is obliged to bail out banks viewed as "too big to fail". In this case, the central bank absorbs part of the risk and, if such action is anticipated, creates a moral hazard in so doing.

Using Robert Lindley's (1998) analysis, a simple but unsatisfactory net settlement system involves:

- End-of-day clearing (or next morning for convenience).
- Settlement of net balances through deposits at the central bank (i.e., with good funds).
- No limits or caps on transfers.
- No collateral or loss-sharing rules.
- Weak or nonexistent legal basis for netting (creating a potential "unwind" problem).[4]
- Poor visibility of risk exposures.

In such a simple system, commercial banks provide implicit credit which is unlimited and unsecured.

A simple RTGS system involves:

- Continuous settlement across accounts at the central bank.
- Unlimited unsecured intraday liquidity from the central bank.
- Finality.

---

[4] An unwind involves undoing all unsettled payments after a participant fails and then redoing the chain of payments as if the participant had not attempted any transactions since the last settlement.

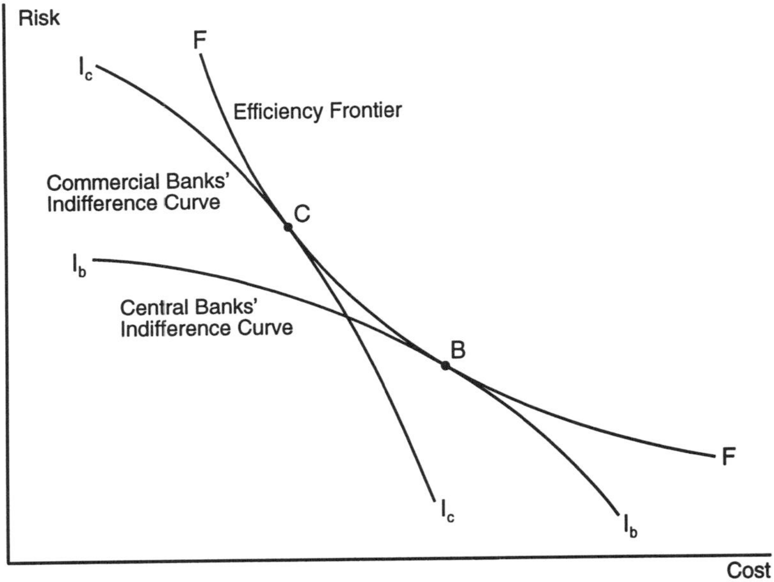

Figure 4.3. Different Central and Commercial Bank Preferences in Terms of Risk–Cost Tradeoffs

An RTGS system is a prerequisite for genuine delivery-versus-payment (DVP) for securities market transactions and payment-versus-payment (PVP) in foreign exchange transactions. But RTGS systems require more liquidity to settle continuous streams of gross payments. To encourage their adoption, central banks may provide this extra liquidity at what appears to be a subsidised price.

There is a perception that the central bank has a preference for a safe but expensive system, while commercial banks prefer a cheaper but riskier system. In terms of the risk–cost tradeoff diagram used in section 4.2 (Figure 4.1), these preferences are illustrated in Figure 4.3, where I_c is the indifference curve between cost and risk for commercial banks and I_b is the indifference curve for the central bank. In this case, commercial banks prefer *C* with greater risk and lower cost to position *B* preferred by the central bank. In some countries, the central bank may impose its preference by dictating a maximum acceptable degree of risk.

Figure 4.4 illustrates an alternative explanation for different choices of commercial and central banks. In this case commercial and central

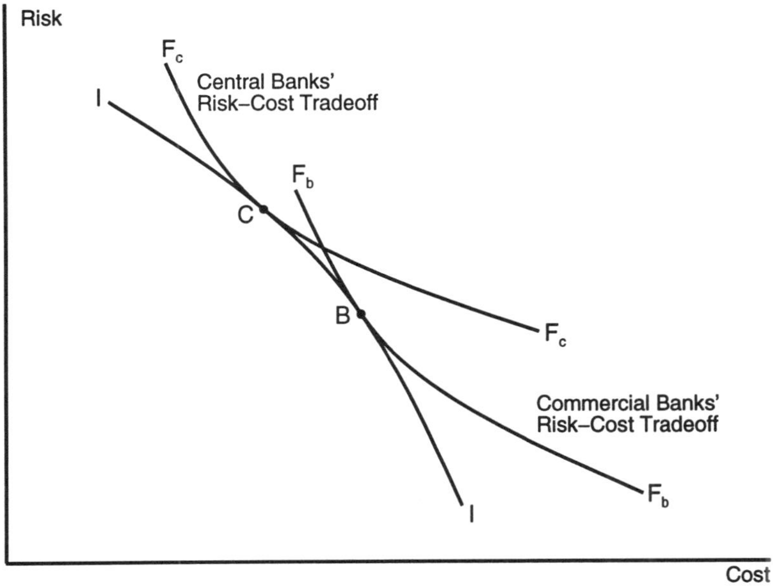

Figure 4.4. Preferences in Terms of Different Central and Commercial Bank Risk–Cost Tradeoffs

banks have the same indifference curve, but commercial banks face a different risk–cost tradeoff F_c from the central bank F_b. In other words, private and social costs differ in Figure 4.4. Commercial banks still prefer *C* with greater risk and lower cost to position *B* preferred by the central bank, but the reason lies not in innate preference towards risk but in some form of price distortion.

Lindley (1998) questions whether this is the crucial difference between DNS and RTGS, i.e., whether they offer a tradeoff between "safe but expensive" and "cheaper but riskier." He argues that the key choice lies in the type of RTGS system adopted. Lindley (1998) bases his case on the observation that liquidity needs in net and gross systems are identical. Table 4.1 illustrates a sequence of payments during the day between bank *A* and bank *B*. It shows that by the fourth payment, bank *A*'s payments to bank *B* have exceeded bank *B*'s payments to bank *A* by 6.

Of crucial importance is the fact that this sequence can occur in either DNS or RTGS systems. Only the type but not the amount of intraday liquidity differs. If this sequence occurred in a DNS system,

Table 4.1. Daily Payment Sequence between Bank A and Bank B

Sequence	*A to B*	*B to A*	*A's Balance*	*B's Balance*
1	3		–3	+3
2	2		–5	+5
3		1	–4	+4
4	2		–6	+6
5		2	–4	+4
6		4	0	0

Maximum overdraft: 6; Average overdraft: 3.8

bank *B* provides liquidity to bank *A* in the form of implicit and free credit. In a protected DNS system, liquidity is provided free but some collateral must be posted. If it is provided at all in an RTGS system, liquidity is invariably provided explicitly by the central bank. The cost of such liquidity depends on reserve requirements, interest on reserve balances, collateral requirements and any interest charged on intraday credit facilities, as discussed at further length in Chapter 7.

Ceteris paribus, risk is harder to control with implicit credit than explicit credit arrangements. Indeed, the provision of implicit credit may be unrecognised or at least unknown. In a paper-based debit transfer system, for example, the net amount of intraday credit provided between banks cannot be known: while bank *A* may know how much it is owed by bank *B*, it cannot know until clearing how much it owes bank *B*. So the provision of free implicit credit is an inevitable component of such a netting system. But if commercial banks are willing to provide intraday free credit in a DNS system, why are they unwilling to do so when operating in an RTGS system if the central bank declines to provide it?

The Swiss National Bank does not provide any intraday liquidity for its RTGS system (SIC). The commercial banks are unwilling to provide intraday liquidity, so the lack of liquidity produces payment queues. Payment instructions submitted to SIC are executed only if the bank has sufficient funds. Otherwise, the payment instruction is queued. Queues are a standard feature of the system and many payments are delayed for several hours. Such delays inevitably introduce settlement risk for some party to the transaction, so destroying one of the main virtues of RTGS. At the end of each day, remaining payment instructions incur a penalty and are cancelled. The alternative is for the commercial banks

Table 4.2. Daily Payment Sequence between Bank A and Bank B with Queue Management

Sequence	*A to B*	*B to A*	*A's Balance*	*B's Balance*
2	2		–2	+2
5		2	0	0
1	3		–3	+3
6		4	+1	–1
4	2		–1	+1
3		1	0	0

Maximum overdraft: 3; Average overdraft: 1.2

to obtain overnight credit from the Swiss National Bank at 2 percent above market.

One solution to this liquidity shortage problem lies in payment management. With payments that require only specific date (value date) but not a specific time for the settlement, Table 4.2 shows that payment prioritisation/queue management can reduce liquidity needs. In this case, which uses the same set of payments as used in Table 4.1, bank *A* needs a balance of 3 rather than the balance of 6 that was required in the previous example where there is no queue management.

Another apparently obvious solution is for bank *B* to provide explicit intraday credit to bank *A*. It does so in the DNS system, so why is it so unwilling to do so in the RTGS system? Why is the preferred solution to delay payments in RTGS systems without central bank liquidity, e.g., in SIC? One answer may lie in the open access to most RTGS systems as opposed to the closed access in many high-value DNS systems. For example, there are over 10,000 participants in FedWire and Germany's CB Express System, while there are only 16 direct settlement banks in CHIPS and CHAPS.[5]

So monitoring of each counterparty's creditworthiness is impossible in the American and German RTGS systems but feasible in both CHAPS and CHIPS. While restrictive membership criteria facilitate risk management, if all settlement members are "too big to fail" the DNS system acquires the ultimate risk protection of the central bank. So one argument in favour of an RTGS system is that it reduces moral hazard and

[5]CHAPS evolved from a DNS to an RTGS system in April 1996.

so improves incentives to monitor counterparty risk. An RTGS system can enhance credibility of the central bank's claim that no bank is too big to fail: failure of even the biggest bank in an RTGS system has no direct implications in terms of credit risk for any other participant.

According to Lindley (1998), RTGS is superior to DNS because:

- It keeps the payment system simple.
- It separates the payment process from liquidity provision.
- The form of liquidity provided (central bank balances, central bank credit, explicit interbank credit) depends on central bank and market preferences.

Dirk Schoenmaker (1995) reaches the opposite conclusion because he assumes that the social costs of liquidity are positive and substantial (Appendix 4.1). However, if a central bank satiates the payment system with liquid assets that banks have to hold for prudential purposes (as in the United Kingdom), this cost evaporates. In such case, the central bank ensures that eligible liquid assets produce the same risk-adjusted yield as all other assets.

Liquidity is economised in a DNS system through the substitution of credit for immediate settlement. As mentioned earlier, a typical large-value net payment system accomplishes $100 in payments for a deferred settlement in "good funds" of $1. Immediate settlement incurs the opportunity cost of holding larger reserve balances (Goodfriend 1991, p. 10). So one way of counteracting commercial banks' reluctance to use a liquidity-intensive RTGS system is for the central bank to subsidise liquidity. As Mark Flannery (1996, p. 807) points out, subsidising transaction costs reduces social welfare.

Flannery's (1996) case against subsidising transaction costs because it reduces social welfare does not hold if private costs of transactions exceed their social costs. Scott Freeman (1996*b*) shows that welfare is maximised when liquidity constraints in a payment system are eliminated through central bank provision of an elastic currency:

> the monetary authority must temporarily supply enough currency to clear all debts at par [a condition that would not occur under liquidity constraints]. This temporary injection of fiat money may take the form of a discount window offering central-bank loans equal to the nominal amount of debt presented to it. Once all debts are cleared, the optimal rediscounting policy requires that the central-bank loans be repaid with fiat money, which is

> then removed from circulation in order to return the fiat-money stock to its initial level, thereby maintaining a constant price level. (Freeman 1996*b*, p. 1127).

> Fiat money is needed both to purchase goods and to repay debt. As a result, the real stock of currency, determined by the demand for money to purchase goods, may be insufficient to permit the unconstrained clearing of credit markets. The selling of debt at a discount indicates a nonoptimal equilibrium. The model of this paper therefore suggests that the optimal central-bank policy includes the elastic provision of a stock of fiat money. Central-bank loans that temporarily increase the stock of central-bank money permit the clearing of debt at par (or at its risk-adjusted price), thus restoring economic efficiency. Therefore, the two roles of money require two distinct central-bank policies: the central bank must not only choose the end-of-period fiat money stock but must also provide within-period central-bank loans sufficient for the clearing of debt unconstrained by a need for liquidity. (Freeman 1996*b*, pp. 1137–1138).

This finding resembles Milton Friedman's (1969) optimum quantity of money. His basic argument is that, because the marginal cost of increasing the real quantity of money is virtually zero, welfare is maximised when real money balances are provided up to the point of satiety. The optimum real quantity of money is that which makes the marginal benefit equal to the zero marginal cost. From the social welfare viewpoint, too much is consumed if private costs fall below social costs and too little if private costs exceed social costs. The optimum quantity of money, i.e., the quantity at which private and social costs are equated at zero, can be achieved by engineering a continuous decrease in the price level. This deflation should reduce the nominal interest rate to zero. Alternatively, the central bank could pay the risk-adjusted nominal interest rate on money balances (Howitt 1992, pp. 81–83). In the case of intraday liquidity, the optimal arrangement from the social welfare perspective is to eliminate liquidity constraints through central bank provision of an elastic supply of liquidity. Then banks will satiate their desire for liquidity for payment purposes because the opportunity cost of holding such liquidity is zero.[6]

For protection against payment risk, the prudential requirements in terms of liquid asset ratios are similar for both RTGS and DNS systems; payment risks are certainly no greater in an RTGS system than they are

[6] Also see Bengt Holmström and Jean Tirole (1998).

in a DNS system. An RTGS system spreads risk more evenly over the day in comparison with a DNS system, which bunches risk at the end of the day.

The form in which liquid assets are held against payment risk is irrelevant, i.e., they serve the same purpose whether they are held as treasury bills or balances in accounts at the central bank. Since the introduction of the United Kingdom's RTGS system in April 1996, the Bank of England has used repurchase agreements to convert banks' liquid assets into payment balances every morning. The Bank sells the assets back to the commercial banks at the same price at the end of the day. In other words, the Bank's intraday interest rate is zero. Because banks must hold these liquid assets for prudential purposes under any alternative payment system arrangements, these intraday balances acquired through intraday repos with the Bank of England incur no additional opportunity costs to satisfy the higher liquidity demands of the RTGS system. In fact, they are well in excess of any likely liquidity needs. While holding liquid assets for prudential purposes is not costless, what is costless is the extra liquidity requirement of the RTGS environment. So the United Kingdom follows the theoretical precepts of Friedman and Freeman in terms of providing costless liquidity for intraday payment purposes.

An alternative way of dealing with this central bank payment risk exposure is to substitute an insurance premium for a liquid asset ratio requirement. Private and social costs of liquidity can still be equated at zero through a zero intraday interest rate. Then a risk premium can be charged appropriately for the risk incurred by the central bank in its provision of intraday liquidity. In effect, this is the Federal Reserve's approach in charging a small fixed interest rate for intraday overdrafts. This interest rate can be considered the risk premium over a zero rate for risk-free intraday liquidity.

4.4 Conclusion

Because the existence of money depends on the existence of uncertainty and transaction costs, a useful framework for analysing payment systems is a variant of the risk-return paradigm used in finance. With cost substituting for return, an efficient payment system can only reduce risk at an increased cost. Where private and social costs diverge, as they do in the case of costly liquidity, central banks can improve social welfare by reducing the cost of liquidity to zero.

Once costs of risk and costs of liquidity are distinguished, the socially optimum strategy appears to be one of providing unlimited intraday liquidity at zero cost but charging a risk premium assessed on each borrower based on standard actuarial principles. This can be achieved either by prudential ratio requirements set on the basis of the payment risk created by each bank or by assessing an insurance premium on users of the payment system.

Appendix 4.1
Schoenmaker's Model

Schoenmaker (1995) considers three types of costs: the cost of settlement failure, the cost of pledging collateral and the cost of payment delay. The cost of collateral is entirely a private cost, but the costs of settlement failure and payment delay take both private and social forms.

Under Schoenmaker's assumption of fully collateralised overdrafts with the central bank, settlement failure involving the cost of covering a possible settlement shortfall can occur only in a net settlement system. The pool of collateral reflecting private cost covers the shortfall up to the amount of collateral posted, after which a social cost is incurred by the central bank to prevent the failure from becoming a systemic crisis.

The second cost in Schoenmaker's model is the opportunity cost of having to pledge collateral. This collateral involves an opportunity cost in that collateral constitutes assets with lower than preferred risk attributes. Furthermore, securities eligible as collateral may incur a substantial liquidity premium unless the payment system is satiated with liquid assets.

The third cost in Schoenmaker's model involving payment delay consists of the cost of preventing such delays and the cost of actual delays. If payments become increasingly time critical, a positive intraday interest rate may constitute the cost of delays. The expected payment delay in an RTGS system is a function of the level of payment reserves, i.e., collateral posted for payment purposes. The private cost of payment delay is a decreasing and convex function of a bank's level of payment reserves divided by its payment flow.

In a net system, payment delay depends on the bank's capacity to send funds and its capacity to receive funds. If a bank sets a low bilateral cap on another bank, incoming payments from that bank may be delayed so, in turn, jeopardising its own ability to send payments. The expected cost of payment delays is a decreasing and convex function of a bank's bilateral cap granted to another bank divided by its payments with that bank. Usually, a bank grants credit lines to those banks that grant it credit lines.

One bank's payment delay may provoke other delays by other banks and eventually produce gridlock. Such gridlock represents an externality or social cost. This social cost of delay is also a decreasing and convex function of the aggregate amount of payment reserves divided by total payment flows in Schoenmaker's model.

Comparing costs under gross and net settlement systems, Schoenmaker (1995) shows that profit maximising behaviour by banks involves setting bilateral credit limits under a net system and deciding the level of collateral under a gross system that minimise private cost. However, banks ignore the externalities of systemic risk and gridlock. This constitutes a rationale for central bank intervention to internalise these externalities.

Optimisation in a gross settlement system involves trading off the cost of extra collateral against the expected cost of payment delays. For a sufficiently high cost of collateral, Schoenmaker (1995, p. 16) shows that, in his model, gridlock is inevitable. In the real world, however, it is difficult to imagine how holding reserves would ever become so costly that the cost of holding reserves deterred payments completely. To reduce the social cost of gridlock, the central bank should make the cost of collateral as low as possible.

In Schoenmaker's (1995) model of a net settlement system, banks must trade off the cost of higher bilateral caps and hence the cost in a loss-sharing arrangement against the cost of payment delays. The central bank offers lender-of-last-resort facilities to surviving banks to prevent systemic failure if the total settlement shortfall exceeds collateral posted. Taking estimates of the various costs in both net and gross payment systems using data for the United States, Schoenmaker (1995, p. 26) concludes that the total cost of gross settlement system is about twice the total cost of a net settlement system. So, assuming risk-neutrality, a net system is preferable on social welfare grounds in this model.

Chapter 5

Reserve Requirements, Liquidity and Risk

5.1 Introduction

IN RECENT YEARS, REQUIRED RESERVES have been reduced or eliminated in many countries, particularly transitional economies, to remove resource allocation distortions and to counteract financial disintermediation. For example, the ratio of bank reserves to bank deposits fell from over 50 percent to under 20 percent in Estonia, 1991–1996, from 25 to 15 percent in Lithuania, 1993–1995, from 35 to 10 percent in Poland, 1988–1996, from 26 to 18 percent in Russia, 1993–1996, and from 80 to 18 percent in the Ukraine, 1992–1997 (*International Financial Statistics*, CD-ROM, March 1997).

To the extent that required reserves can be used during the day for payment purposes, they provide a costless source of liquidity. But noninterest-earning required reserves impose negative effective protection on a country's financial system so encouraging residents to use cheaper financial intermediation services abroad. International competition is therefore forcing monetary authorities to reduce the burden of reserve requirements either by lowering ratios or by paying interest on such reserves. At the same time, RTGS systems have been introduced in many industrial, transitional and developing countries both to eliminate settlement risk from high-value payment systems and to reduce moral hazard.

These two tendencies create potential friction: the former diminishes demand for reserves to be kept overnight and the latter increases demand for reserves during the day. This conflict may encourage banks to spend too much effort from the social welfare viewpoint in managing their reserves. This chapter describes and discusses ways of dealing with these opposing forces, particularly as they apply to transitional and developing countries.

The analysis in this chapter concludes that:

- Paying interest on both required and excess reserves has advantages for the payment system and, in many circumstances, facilitates some aspects of the implementation of monetary policy.
- Central facilities to manage queues for pending payments in RTGS systems can be useful whenever there is limited liquidity.
- A prudential liquid asset requirement can help ensure that there is a clear distinction between central bank intraday liquidity provision and lender-of-last-resort activities.

5.2 Basic Intermediate Monetary Policy Targets

The basic intermediate targets of monetary policy analysed here are:[1]

- The short-term interest rate.
- The exchange rate.
- The level of bank reserves.

Central banks can set a ceiling on the short-term interest rate by discounting bank assets, by taking securities in repurchase agreements, etc. They can always set a floor for the short-term interest rate by accepting deposits at that rate, by paying interest on reserves, etc.

Alternatively, central banks can set a floor on the exchange rate of a target currency by buying it at a set price, increasing reserve money in the process. If at the same time a central bank attempts to keep interest rates up, it may have to buy more foreign currency and the cost of maintaining foreign exchange reserves may increase. To maintain a ceiling on the exchange rate of a target currency, a central bank has to stand ready to sell it at a set price, thereby draining reserve money from the system. If this central bank attempts to keep interest rates down,

[1] Many central banks do not have such well-defined intermediate monetary policy targets.

demand for foreign exchange will increase and the central bank may lose all its foreign exchange reserves.

Finally, central banks can influence the level of bank reserves by supplying credits, accepting deposits, entering into repurchase agreements and by buying and selling securities. Some central banks use administrative controls to prohibit banks from engaging in certain activities. Here we ignore such practices because they raise too many issues that are not central to this study.

Central banks that set a precise target for the global level of bank reserves usually establish reserve requirements high enough to facilitate payments. Alternatively, they provide overdrafts and treat these as negative reserve balances when computing the period-average reserve holdings. To ignore such overdrafts because they appeared in separate accounts would clearly defeat the objective of reserve targeting.

If the central bank's intermediate monetary policy target is either to keep the level of bank reserves within some range or to maintain an exchange rate against a target currency, there may be large fluctuations in the overnight interest rate at the end of the day or of the reserve maintenance period. If an efficient money market exists, whenever there is any surplus over required reserves, the overnight rate at the end the day or of the reserve maintenance period should fall to the rate, if any, paid by the central bank on excess reserves. Conversely, whenever there is a reserve shortage at the end of the day or of the reserve maintenance period, the overnight rate should rise to the cost of having a reserve deficit for a few transactions.

However, central banks that seek to control the exchange rate are in a better position to accept these fluctuations, since it is much easier for most people to understand the advantages of exchange rate stability than those of bank reserve stability. In both cases, paying interest on excess reserves helps reduce interest rate volatility at the end of the day or reserve maintenance period because this interest rate provides a floor to market interest rates. The closer the rate paid on excess reserves is to the market interest rate, the closer should be the end-of-day or end-of-reserve-maintenance-period rate to the normal market rate.

Central banks that target the level of bank reserves usually try to achieve the objective by influencing short-term interest rates. However, it is possible to lose control over short-term interest rates when targeting bank reserves. Situations can exist and have existed where large players have attempted and even succeeded in cornering the reserve market. Short-term interest rates may also be influenced by efforts to deliberately incur a shortfall in required reserves. It is clearly in the interests of the central bank to deter such practices in one way or another.

5.3 Reserves and the Payment System

Before central banks embraced the role of lender of last resort, commercial banks held reserves to meet withdrawals, to make payments and because even a rumour about a reserve shortage could trigger a run on them by depositors. One of the original reasons for establishing central banks was to pool reserves to make banks more secure and at the same time to reduce the amount of reserves banks needed to hold (Bagehot 1873).

In the early days of central banking, banks were required to hold reserves both for prudential reasons and for monetary control. Recently reserve requirements have been reduced in France, Japan, Sweden and the United States, and eliminated in Belgium, Canada, Kuwait, Mexico, Norway, Switzerland and the United Kingdom. So now some banks hold reserves only by accident. These banks depend heavily on interbank credit and the money market to settle their payments and to dispose of any excess reserves. However, reserves can be useful to payment systems. In particular, in countries where central bank intraday overdrafts are not granted or overnight overdrafts are severely penalised, banks need to keep some reserves to settle their payments. Three basic approaches to meeting the demand for reserves are discussed in the following sections. A country can also adopt any combination of these approaches.

5.3.1 Reserve requirements

Required reserve regimes were imposed to control the size of some monetary aggregate rather than for payment purposes. However, most countries using reserve requirements allow these reserves to provide liquidity for the payment system, as shown by the questionnaire results. To free reserves for payment purposes, banks are usually allowed to meet their requirements on an average basis over some maintenance period as, for example, in Poland, Tanzania and the United States.

Table 5.1 shows some characteristics of reserve requirements across the BoE group. In general, required reserves are least burdensome for the commercial banks in industrial countries, where several countries impose no requirements, and most burdensome for banks in developing

Table 5.1. Reserve Requirements in the Bank of England Group (average percent or percent of countries in each group)

Characteristic	*Industrial*	*Transitional*	*Developing*
Required reserve ratio	4	11	9
Separate account	13	40	67
Interest paid	50	36	16
Available for payments	82	82	65
Maintenance period			
1 day	13	22	7
1 week	13	0	46
2 weeks	14	33	7
1 month	60	45	36

Required reserve ratios	–	Mean required reserve ratio across each country group.
Separate account	–	Percentage of countries in each group where required reserves must be held in a separate account at the central bank.
Interest paid	–	Percentages of countries in each group that pay interest on required reserves.
Available for payments	–	Percentage of countries in each group that permit required reserves to be used during the day for payment purposes.
Maintenance period	–	Percentages of countries in each group using one of four maintenance periods.

countries, where they often serve as an important source of government revenue (Fry 1997, Ch. 2). Few industrial countries require separate accounts for required reserves in contrast to the majority of developing countries that do. Twice as many industrial countries than developing countries pay interest on required reserves. Most industrial countries permit banks to use required reserves for payment purposes, while only just over half the developing countries allow such use. Finally, 60 percent of industrial countries impose the longest one-month average period compared to 40 percent of developing countries.

5.3.2 Frequent intervention by the central bank

The central bank can inject reserves when they are needed and drain them at the end of the day. Alternatively, it can provide some automatic overnight credit at reasonable rates to banks that post suitable collateral or that are sound. However, frequent intervention may thwart the development of money markets and generate socially inefficient administrative costs.

5.3.3 Paying interest on reserves

In the United States, the Federal Reserve eliminated reserve requirements on nontransaction deposits in 1990. Because banks then found managing their liquidity needs for payment purposes much harder, the Federal Reserve Bank of New York began searching for ways to deal with these difficulties (Federal Reserve Bank of New York 1993). That work dealt with several issues that arise in the payment system. One of the recommendations was to pay interest on required reserves rather than to lower the required reserve ratio (Hilton, Gerdts and Robinson 1993). Besides reducing the opportunity cost of a potentially important source of payment system liquidity, interest paid on required reserves also deters banks from evading reserve requirements by switching to liabilities that are not subject to them and from lobbying for reductions in the percentage required.

The New York Fed's recommendation appears to be valid for many other countries that have reserve requirements and a reasonably efficient tax collecting system. Requiring banks to keep reserve money without paying them interest is a form of taxation that produces undesirable distortions in the allocation of resources. It should generally be possible to find better ways of raising revenue. Also, in some countries unremunerated reserve requirements give advantages to nonbanks—institutions that may not be regulated or as well regulated as banks—over banks in providing financial services.

The New York Fed study also discusses paying interest on excess reserves. It does not recommend this practice for the United States because of the characteristics of the discount window and because some other instruments are available to increase bank reserves and to facilitate settling payments.[2] However, paying interest on excess reserves has many advantages:

---

[2]The Federal Reserve already pays interest on "Clearing Balance Accounts." These accounts are kept to allow banks to lower the opportunity costs of keeping reserves to settle payments. Banks can set an amount to be maintained in this regime and they are administered in a way that is very similar as the one used for reserve requirements. For banks that use this option, the effect of this is similar to a reserve requirement increase with interest paid on the added required reserves.

- It dampens fluctuations in overnight interest rates by setting a floor on them.
- It provides incentives for banks to maintain a pool of lendable funds that makes it easier for banks to square their accounts at the end of the day or of the reserve maintenance period.
- It makes it much harder for a financial institution to corner the market.
- It provides a buffer for the overnight rate and so requires much less frequent intervention by the central bank.
- Interest paid on excess reserves need not be costly to the central bank, but could even provide it with a source of revenue. The central bank can pay an interest rate lower than the market rate, invest the reserves at the market rates and use the spread to offset expenses and market risk.

Therefore, paying interest on excess reserves can be a valuable device that should be carefully considered to make the payment systems more efficient. The rest of this section discusses some ideas to help evaluate this option.

A central bank thinking about paying interest on reserve balances needs to examine the mechanism that would generate the demand for excess reserves. It seems reasonable to assume that banks would seek to minimise the expected costs of maintaining reserves. Perhaps the simplest way to do this is to use a model known to mathematical programmers as the newsboy problem. This model deals with random shortages or surpluses, where both surpluses and shortages have independent costs proportional to size. In the case of bank reserves, a bank determines the level of reserves it wants at the end of the day or reserve maintenance period. At the end of the period, the bank has to cover the cost of any reserve deficit or incur the opportunity cost of any excess reserves. For each bank, the margin of error on final reserve levels may depend on late payments received or ordered by customers, the efficiency of the money market, its access to it, currency demand, the forecasting ability of the central bank and the frequency of its intervention, etc.

The very existence of excess reserves would increase the money market's efficiency and reduce any incentives banks may have to delay sending payments. These are factors that reduce the uncertainty on final reserve balances and, in turn, the need to keep excess reserves. A central

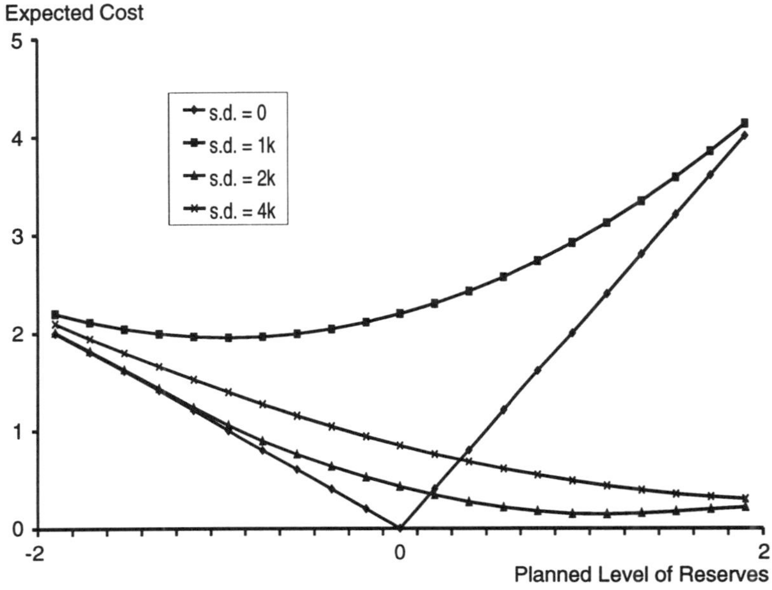

Figure 5.1. Expected Costs of Holding Reserves with Different Standard Deviations

bank would have to find an equilibrium by slowly providing excess reserves to the banks, adjusting the interest rate on excess reserves and the penalty for reserves shortages. The cost of holding excess reserves is roughly the market rate minus the interest rate paid, while the cost of a reserve shortage is the penalty rate minus the market rate.

Figure 5.1 plots expected costs for four banks with different standard deviations of their end-of-day reserve balances as a function of the reserves they intend to keep. One bank has perfect control over its final reserves, a standard deviation of zero, and the others expects errors with probability distributions of the same shape but with standard deviation of 1, 2 and 4. In this example, the cost of a reserve shortfall is 10 times the cost of a reserve surplus.

Figure 5.1 illustrates some properties of this model that are consistent with some simple generalisations about a bank's reserve management problem:

- For any bank, the level of reserves with a minimum expected cost increases with the ratio of the cost of a deficit over the cost of a surplus.

- If the cost of a deficit is greater than the cost of a surplus and the uncertainty about the level of reserves for a group of banks is modelled by a class of probability distributions with the standard deviation as the only parameter, then the level of reserves with a minimum expected cost grows with the standard deviation. The expected cost for one bank is never larger than the expected cost for another bank with a larger standard deviation.

- If the cost of a surplus is zero and the probability distribution has a bounded range, then a large but finite level of reserves has an expected cost of zero.

- If the cost of maintaining reserves is the same as that of having a deficit, as would happen if no interest were paid on excess reserves and the penalty rate charged for reserve deficits or overnight overdrafts is twice the market rate, then the level of intended reserves with a minimum expected cost is zero. This conclusion is based on a probability distribution such that the probability of having more reserves than the intended level is equal to that of having less.

From these properties, a central bank may use the following guidelines to establish the optimum interest rate on excess reserves:

- The rate paid on excess reserves should be significantly lower than market rates. If rates are too close to market levels, the cost function becomes flat around the minimum and banks may chose to keep too many excess reserves, endangering the central bank's monetary control. For countries where market rates are low, it may be perfectly reasonable not to pay interest on reserves and still expect banks to hold a sufficient amount of excess reserves.

- Monetary control can be enhanced by setting a limit for each bank on the amount of interest paid in any day for excess reserves. This measure would make the expected cost of holding excess reserves increase more than proportionally as the intended level of reserves rises.

- The cost of a reserve deficit should be significantly higher than the cost of a surplus. Otherwise, banks would not keep any excess reserves and the added liquidity for the money market would not materialise. In countries with reserve requirements, a steeper penalty rate can be charged for overdrafts than for reserve deficits. More generally, the penalty rate for deficits can be an increasing function of the size of the reserve deficit.

An interest rate that is a function of lagged market interest rates may limit the central bank's ability to lower interest rates quickly. Any such rule would set a floor to future interest rates. However, rules can be written to ensure that interest rates can drop very fast, so this should not cause problems. In some countries, it may be difficult to establish precisely what market rates are. In such cases, a floor for interest rates appears useful, even if it differs from perceptions about what the market rate is or should be.

5.4 Intraday Credit

5.4.1 The central bank as provider of intraday credit

Central banks are the ultimate source of liquidity and have a clear interest in promoting the sound development of the payment system. So in most circumstances, it makes sense that they should grant intraday credit, as this allows efficient settlement of payments with reasonable costs and low risks for participants. On the other hand, central banks have to ensure that they do not lose monetary control and that moral hazard is kept at low levels.

Each central bank should consider carefully the effect of a failure by the banks to repay this intraday credit. In particular, a central bank should examine what would happen should the financial system come under stress. Also, it should keep in mind the characteristics of its country, as most of the available literature on payment systems has been written in advanced countries by people who take for granted a sound banking infrastructure, reasonable banking supervision and may not be fully aware of conditions elsewhere. Other countries may face completely different risks and need an even more cautious central bank.

A basic fact that should never be overlooked is that intraday credit has the potential of becoming overnight credit. The debtor can obtain an overnight credit simply by not repaying the intraday credit at the end of the day. Giving banks an overdraft facility or granting them credit via automatic repurchase agreement creates central bank reserves until the credit is repaid.

Central banks should be careful not to accept too much risk from the banks to themselves. Intraday credit should have strict limits if uncollateralised or appropriate collateral in order to protect the central bank from excessive credit risk as well as to curb moral hazard.

In this study, we suppose that intraday liquidity is injected by allowing banks to enter into automatic intraday repurchase agreements with the central bank. This is roughly equivalent to allowing them collateralised overdrafts, although there may be significant legal differences. The central bank should accept as collateral for intraday credit a range of securities (eligible assets) wide enough so that there is an adequate supply of them to make settlement of payments efficient under an RTGS system.

Intraday liquidity provision might be described as an activity where the central bank is the lender of first resort. This function should be clearly separated from the central bank's classic role of lender of last resort. Credits granted in this latter role should not in any sense be automatic; credit officers should be involved both in the granting of the loan and in subsequent monitoring.

5.4.2 Haircuts on eligible assets

Collateral taken for intraday credit should protect the central bank from credit risk. Since the market value of the securities taken as collateral can fall in value, it is important to assign them a collateral value below their market value. The difference is known as a haircut, and it should be large enough to make it highly probable that the securities will not fall in value below the amount of the intraday credit. If the intermediate monetary policy target of the central bank is to keep short-term interest rates within bounds, haircuts are easy to calculate for securities with a short-term to maturity or with adjustable rates, since the value of these securities does not change much. However, for longer-term securities, the effects of a major rise in interest rates should be considered.

For central banks whose intermediate monetary policy target is to keep the exchange rate for a target currency within bounds, the problem of determining adequate haircuts is rather more difficult. The value of even very short-term securities can fall rapidly during a currency attack by speculators, so central banks have to be particularly careful when setting haircuts under this monetary policy regime.

Finally, central banks should consider the value or danger of haircuts as signals to the market.

5.4.3 Limits on uncollateralised central bank intraday credit

Prudence dictates that limits should be placed on any central bank intraday credit that is not fully covered by collateral. These limits should be carefully set by the central bank considering the size of each bank, its management and other relevant characteristics.

5.4.4 Costs of intraday credit facilities

The costs incurred by the central bank when providing intraday liquidity are:

- Receiving, processing and registering intraday repurchase agreements or receiving collateral for overdrafts that incur some transaction costs.
- The haircut on the value of the securities may be insufficient to cover the loss in value of the securities in a crisis. Some issuers may default. Either event exposes the central bank to credit risk.

Only the costs on the first item can be readily estimated and central banks usually charge these to the users of its electronic systems. Costs of bank failures and defaults involve estimating probabilities for such events and will involve subjective elements. The cost of failing to achieve an intermediate monetary policy target is also difficult to gauge, since it is hard to determine its effect on achieving the central bank's ultimate goal. Nevertheless, it is appropriate to charge these costs to banks in the form of higher haircuts and as penalties to banks that actually go into overdraft. Since the banks already face the costs of collateralised intraday credit described in the following paragraph and since the central bank has a clear interest in promoting efficiency in the payment system, it is important not to overestimate the risk the central bank faces.

Banks incur costs of collateralised intraday credit. Banks are in the business of taking some risks and they can usually achieve better results holding assets that are not as liquid and secure as eligible assets. Extensive use of these eligible assets as collateral increases demand for them and this will probably lower their yields. This effect is particularly important if eligible assets are in short supply and if a significant fraction of these securities in circulation is needed as collateral for intraday credit. This situation also affects other buyers of eligible assets, who in turn gain even more liquidity. The issuers of eligible assets capture these expenses.

Central banks may issue eligible assets to capture some or all the benefits. If they issue all eligible assets, they can also control the maximum amount of intraday credit they extend, should they deem this appropriate. This monopoly should not be used to maximise income, as it could make the payment system inefficient, inducing participants to delay payments and to spend too much effort managing their liquidity. Delays on payments and higher costs for banks could result in a significant reduction in social welfare.

As a benchmark to guide the rationing of intraday facilities, it seems reasonable to encourage the development of an intraday market for liquidity that uses interbank repurchase agreements with a wider range of securities. Such a market would tell the central bank how the market prices intraday liquidity and the risk of default.

5.5 Liquid Asset Requirements

Some countries require banks to keep liquid assets. Since few events can damage trust as much as banks not settling their obligations on time, such a requirement seems a sensible element of the banking supervisory framework. Banks depend on their reputation to remain in business and confidence is extremely important to the financial system. The definition of assets that qualify to fulfil the liquid asset requirement should include assets that are eligible for the intraday credit facility, but it could include a wider range of other assets. For some banks active in the financial markets and with few short-term obligations, the amount of eligible assets they keep may be larger than their required liquid assets.

The rules for setting the amount of required liquid assets should be based on the size of the bank, the composition of its clientele, etc. One way to protect banks from liquidity risks is to require them to have enough very liquid assets to cover outflows for a set number of days, in the event that the perception of the bank deteriorates so it is not able to get interbank loans or issue paper in the securities market, and it loses its large sight deposits and even some of its retail deposit base. The number of days covered by these liquid assets should be sufficient to enable the central bank to decide whether to act as a lender of last resort, to set appropriate terms for such loans or to confront the possibility of systemic risk if it decides not to rescue the troubled bank.

Banks should be able to liquidate all liquid assets at any time, as liquid assets that cannot be sold when needed are hardly liquid. However, any shortfall of required liquid assets should be reported immediately to the central bank to avoid surprises. The central bank should ask the bank for an explanation and a plan to recoup liquid assets to the required level. A penalty proportional to the deficit on liquid assets would lead banks to keep extra liquid assets in the same way that penalties on reserve shortfalls can encourage excess reserve holding.

The requirement to maintain liquid assets has some characteristics similar to a regime of required reserves with interest, but the rate would be determined directly by the market and the banks would have some freedom in choosing and maintaining their portfolios. Moreover, the use of averaging does not seem an appropriate feature of what is a prudential rather than a monetary control-related requirement.

5.6 Centralised Queue Management

Unless intraday liquidity is virtually free, banks need queues in an RTGS system to manage outgoing payments when they do not have enough reserves to settle them immediately. They may also need to conserve liquidity for their most time-critical payments. Banks may have their own internal payment queuing/scheduling arrangements. Where intraday liquidity is costly, however, most RTGS systems provide central queuing facilities.

Management of central queues enables banks to minimise intraday liquidity needs and may also help reduce the length of time that payments are delayed in queues. Such management may take the form of reordering payments in the queue, e.g., moving a payment at the top of the queue that is blocking payments behind it to the bottom of the queue or, in its more complicated form, running an optimisation routine that identifies a subset of queued payments that, if all were settled simultaneously, would leave all banks concerned with nonnegative balances or within-limit overdrafts.

Degrees of queue transparency differ markedly across different RTGS systems. If banks are given up-to-date information not just on their settlement account balances but also on the payments queued for them to receive, this can assist them in their liquidity management. However, a major argument against providing information on queued payments to banks is that it may reintroduce settlement risk: banks may be tempted to act on a queued payment instruction by giving the ultimate payee access to the incoming funds before that payment has been settled. Restricting queued payment information, e.g., by providing information only on aggregate queued payments, may avoid this problem. While not normal practice in RTGS systems, allowing queued payments to be revoked may also discourage banks from treating queued payments as if they had already been settled.

In any event, it may be difficult not to conclude that queues negate some of the advantages of an RTGS system: settling payments that have been delayed for hours hardly qualifies as "real time" and reintroduces the settlement risks that true RTGS removes.

5.7 Conclusion

Increased international competition for financial intermediation business and heightened awareness of the distortionary effects of required reserves have led to lower required reserve ratios in many countries. From the perspective of payment efficiency, we find considerable merit both in allowing such reserves to be used as a source of intraday liquidity and in paying competitive interest rates on required and excess reserves. The existence of liquid asset ratios for prudential purposes can also increase the pool of assets that may be mobilised intraday for the provision of payment system liquidity.

Central bank liquidity provision should not transfer undue risk from the commercial banks to the central bank. So, in virtually all circumstances, central bank credit for all maturities should be collateralised. Furthermore, reasonable administrative costs involved in central bank provision of liquidity should be borne by the commercial banks. However, such charges should not be seen as a source of profit and should be held to a minimum in order not to deter banks from using an RTGS system in preference to a DNS payment system.

Every study on payment systems focusing on the problems faced by developing and transitional countries should include a discussion of moral hazard. When the G-10 countries started studying payment systems, they were searching for ways to decrease systemic risk. They failed to stress, perhaps because it was obvious to them, that the central bank can easily decrease or eliminate systemic risk if it is willing to assume risks banks face in the settlement of payments. This is clearly undesirable because it increases moral hazard.

Central bank support to the payment system in the form of automatic and *unsecured* liquidity provision may allow banks to keep operating longer than they should from the prudential viewpoint. It may also make banks too dependent on the central bank and eliminate incentives for them to hold liquid assets. Too much unsecured central bank support may reduce banks' readiness to monitor the creditworthiness of other participants in deferred net settlement systems. It may deter banks from developing an interbank credit market and from participating actively in the securities market, so ensuring that these markets remain thin and illiquid. At worst, ill-conceived central bank support for the payment system may not only create excessive moral hazard but also impair monetary control.

As an example, consider a central bank that guarantees the settlement of a cheque clearing house, i.e., the central bank will credit the accounts of banks with a net credit position and allow any overdraft on the accounts of banks with a net debit position. A bank could raise reserves and pay for them with a certified cheque to be presented through the clearing house. The cheque would be very good collateral, but such an arrangement would ensure that, whenever the bank has problems, it will end up a debtor of the central bank. Other sources of moral hazard occur when large overdrafts not totally collateralised are permitted and haircuts for the collateral eligible for use in automatic credit facilities are inadequate.

Chapter 6

Central Bank Roles in Payment Systems

6.1 Introduction

CENTRAL AND COMMERCIAL BANKERS now generally realise that payment and settlement arrangements cannot simply be left for the "back office" to sort out. In their role as the "plumbing" of the financial and banking system, the efficiency and safety of these arrangements have become issues with wider strategic and policy implications for central banks.[1] So this chapter has two basic objectives. The first is to examine the reasons why central banks are interested in payment systems. The second is to provide an overview of the role of central banks in the payment system reforms in transitional economies; Poland is used for illustrative purposes.

By way of illustration, the Bank of England's mission statement specifically recognises the promotion of sound and efficient payment and settlement arrangements as an important element of the Bank's core purposes. Gerry Corrigan, former President of the Federal Reserve Bank of New York, also recognised this important role when referring to the "trilogy" of central banking functions and responsibilities: monetary policy, banking supervision and payment systems.

---

[1] Andrew Crockett (1998, p. 4) points out that the BIS Committee on Payment and Settlement Systems was transformed into a senior-level body in 1990 after the growing realisation that "payment systems were not only a technical matter but also went to the very heart of central bank policy concerns."

Table 6.1. Central Bank Ownership of Payment Systems (percent of countries in each group)

Type of Ownership	*Industrial*	*Transitional*	*Developing*
	Real-Time Gross Settlement Systems		
Sole	56	86	100
Joint	6	14	0
None	38	0	0
	Deferred Net Settlement Systems		
Sole	6	44	47
Joint	44	44	37
None	50	12	16

6.2 Central Bank Ownership and Oversight of Payment Systems

Table 6.1 records ownership of the major payment systems across the BoE group. Ownership is particularly important to the extent that payment systems pool or absorb participants' payment risks. Unsurprisingly, there is considerably less central bank ownership of payment systems in the industrial countries than in the transitional and developing countries. While 62 percent of central banks in industrial countries own or part-own their country's RTGS systems, central banks in transitional and developing countries own or part-own all the existing RTGS systems. Similarly, 50 percent of DNS systems in industrial countries are entirely privately owned, but a large majority of DNS systems in transitional and developing countries are owned or part-owned by their central banks.

Table 6.2 provides a summary of central bank oversight of the payment systems in the BoE group. The majority of central banks in all three groups possess formal powers of oversight over their country's payment systems, a minority use informal arrangements, while some exert both formal and informal powers. Comparing Tables 6.1 and 6.2 demonstrates that only in the industrial countries is strong formal oversight responsibility not reflected fully in the central banks' operational involvement.

Table 6.3 shows the questionnaire answers on pricing of central bank payment services. Central banks in the industrial countries tend to price

Table 6.2. Central Bank Oversight over Payment Systems (percent of countries in each group)

Type of Oversight	*Industrial*	*Transitional*	*Developing*
Formal	50	77	70
Informal	25	23	21
Both	25	0	9

Table 6.3. Pricing of Central Bank Payment Services (percent of countries in each group)

Type of Pricing	*Industrial*	*Transitional*	*Developing*
Free	5	8	61
Subsidised	0	25	3
Full-cost recovery	90	42	27
Target rate of return	0	17	0
Other	5	8	9

their services on the basis of full-cost recovery, whereas central banks in developing countries typically provide their services free of charge. The distortions so created may appear small at present. Experience from the industrial countries suggests, however, that the sooner such distortions are removed, the less likely are a country's inhabitants to fall into expensive and socially inefficient habits, such as writing cheques for sums smaller than the costs of the cheque processing.

6.3 Increasing Central Bank Involvement in Payment Systems

As suggested in the introduction, central banks have tended to play a more active role in payment systems since the late 1970s than they did in earlier years. In large part, this is due to rapid technological changes, dramatic growth of financial activity and the consequent enormous growth in both volumes and values of payment transactions, and the integration or globalisation of financial markets. As a result liquidity and credit risks for central banks, commercial banks and other participants involved in payment systems have increased dramatically. Furthermore, payment systems have become a serious potential source of domestic and cross-border financial crises.

In this new environment, promoting stability and efficiency of payment systems, developing measures to reduce risk and ensuring that payment system arrangements and changes in such arrangements do not jeopardise monetary management have become crucial central bank objectives. The efficiency of a country's payment system is one determinant of its rate of economic growth. Here the speed and certainty of fund transfers from the payer's account to the payee's account are the key elements.

Central banks can promote such efficiency in two primary ways—by operational involvement or via oversight. As shown in the questionnaire answers from the BoE group, the degree to which central banks are involved in operational activities differs across countries. Nevertheless, there is a tendency for central banks to play a more active role in developing and running large-value transfer systems than in small-value transfer systems. Quite apart from operational involvement, however, all central banks perform some degree of payment system oversight. In some countries, this amounts to a formal regulatory role for the central bank often involving responsibility for developing the rules for the operation of the payment system(s). In others, central bank influences are less formal, with day-to-day management of the payment system undertaken by the commercial banks. Where commercial banks have existed for centuries, central banks tend to play a more passive role than they do in countries that until recently possessed a monobanking system.

In general, central bank interest in the stability of payment systems is manifested in attempts to reduce the probability of a large participant in the payment system becoming unable to meet its obligations. Such inability can cause serious difficulties for the safe functioning of the system and for other participants. Reducing this risk, known as systemic risk, is the primary central bank objective in the field of payment systems.

In implementing monetary policy, central banks pursue intermediate targets such as growth rates of monetary aggregates or, in many cases, short-term interest rates. On the one hand, the effectiveness of indirect instruments of monetary policy depends on the stage of development of the financial markets that are used to transmit monetary policy signals. On the other hand, the type of payment instruments used in payment systems, the payment facilities available for market participants as well as the rules and procedures for payments influence the speed, risk and cost of transactions in financial markets. For example, while open market operations necessitate well-developed markets, they also require payment and settlement systems that can transfer securities through book entries and settle transactions accurately, speedily and with finality.

Some central bank objectives with respect to the country's payment system may be incompatible with others. For example, one way of reducing systemic risk is to adopt an RTGS system. However, such adoption may have implications for monetary policy implementation. One important issue here—discussed at some length in Chapters 4 and 5—involves the cost of liquidity. There are also issues relating to intraday overdrafts for RTGS payments, pricing and guaranteeing payment finality. The choice of payment system may involve a tradeoff between risk reduction and the effectiveness of monetary policy. A further linkage between payment systems and monetary policy instruments arises in the case of reserve requirements. Since such reserves can usually be used for settlements during the day, they contribute to the smooth functioning of the payment system. Furthermore, changes in payment systems can cause changes in the velocity of money and banks' demand for reserves. So central banks must take such changes into account when implementing monetary policy.

Another important issue relating to the general efficiency of payment systems, particularly the efficiency with which they enable monetary policy to be implemented, is payment float. Float is created, in the main, because of delays in the execution of payment transactions. More specifically, it arises because of delays between the respective debiting and crediting of payer and payee in the payment process. This produces purely incidental and, from an efficiency viewpoint, undesirable gains and losses for the parties concerned.

There are two kinds of float—credit float and debit float. Credit float is created when a bank debits a client's account before transferring the funds to the beneficiary's bank or when the receiving bank delays the crediting of the beneficiary's account. Credit float represents effectively an interest-free loan from bank customers to their banks, so banks have an incentive to delay the processing and crediting of payments to customer accounts (Veale and Price 1994, p. 147). Debit float arises from the processing of cheques or other debit instruments, when a bank credits the payee before receiving money from the payer's bank or when the payer's account is debited with delay after funds are paid to the payee's bank. In this case, bank customers receive the benefit of float at the expense of the banks.

Table 6.4. Credit and Debit Float

Relationship	*Credit Float*	*Debit Float*
Commercial banks and their customers	Generated by credit payments such as giro or payment orders. The commercial bank benefits at the expense of the customer.	Generated by debit payments such as cheques. Customers benefit at the expense of commercial banks.
Central bank and commercial banks	Generated by credit payments when the account of the payer bank at the central bank is debited before the account of the payee bank is credited. The central bank benefits at the expense of the commercial banks because commercial bank reserves are decreased.	Generated by debit payments when the account of the payer bank at the central bank is debited after the account of the payee bank is credited. The commercial banks benefit at the expense of the central bank because commercial bank reserves are increased.

Source: Veale and Price (1994, Table 1, p. 151).

Both kinds of float can also exist in the central bank/commercial bank account relationship. Inefficient processing of transfers by the central bank could cause the delay, e.g., when instructions have to be transmitted from one central bank branch to another. Hence, commercial banks may provide interest-free loans to the central bank if the central bank debits the account of a bank instructing it to transfer funds before crediting the payee bank's account. Conversely, the central bank provides an interest-free loan to the banking system when it credits a bank's account for funds owed before it debits the payer bank's account. In any event, one of the parties to a payment transaction is either granting or receiving interest-free credit. John Veale and Robert Price (1994, p. 149) construct the matrix reproduced in Table 6.4 distinguishing credit/debit and central bank–bank/bank–customer float.

The volume of float can be important for several reasons. For example, lenders may be unable to charge borrowers for the credit they have extended, borrowers can decide when and how much they borrow and banks may use float to cover some of their costs. From the central bank's viewpoint, float can affect the level and volatility of banks' reserves and complicate the operation of monetary policy. Central banks have a strong preference to minimise payment float, especially in industrial countries where the principle of time value of money (TVM) is well understood. Typically, central banks attempt to reduce float by accelerating paper processing procedures and introducing funds' availability schedules.

The effectiveness of a payment system is also vital for financial stability. Disruption in the payment system reduces public confidence in the financial sector. So to maintain confidence in the financial sector, the central bank must promote a sound and efficient payment system. The payment system constitutes one source of risk to commercial banks. Liquidity problems of one of the participants may cause problems for other participants and so for the entire system.

On the one hand, timely information from the payment system may provide warning signals. On the other hand, some information about an individual bank may produce reactions that exacerbate the difficulty if published by the supervisory authorities. Hence, cooperation between payment system and supervisory specialists is essential. Such cooperation can help central banks to distinguish between serious problems, which may cause insolvency, and temporary liquidity problems. For example, central banks usually have information about whether a commercial bank is experiencing difficulty in maintaining reserve balances at the required level and about its reliance on intraday credit to fund payments.

Although reducing systemic risk has been an important central bank objective for some years, central banks have also been concerned about the relationship between payment arrangements and monetary policy. This springs from the fact that the first link in the transmission mechanism of monetary policy involves payments of one kind or another. Hence, the efficiency of the payment system is essential for monetary policy implementation and for its effective transmission through the economy.

The increasing volume and value of transactions through their payment systems in many economies explain why central banks have become increasing involved in payment system issues in recent years. But is this true for all countries? Perhaps only central banks in industrial countries with developed financial sectors and strong economies that are integrated into the global economy focus on their countries' payment systems. To what extent are central banks in transitional and developing countries involved in their payment systems? What is the effect of different levels of central bank involvement in payment systems? What are the common approaches of central banks to their payment systems?

Views on the role that central banks should play in payment systems are diverse, in large part because different conditions in each country —differences in payment instruments, the domestic financial sector, legal systems, technical infrastructure, stage of institutional development, country size, etc.—make each payment system unique. So in some countries central banks are active providers of payment services, competing with commercial banks, while in other countries, such as Slovenia and the United Kingdom, central banks do not play such a role.

The Federal Reserve Banks of the United States provide a wide variety of payment services that include collection of cheque payments, electronic fund transfers, securities transfer and custodial services for government securities. The Deutsche Bundesbank makes its payment systems available to all credit institutions, many of which operate their own giro systems. The Bundesbank operates an RTGS system (ELS) as well as a liquidity-saving system (EAF), which combines gross and net features, for large-value payments. The Bundesbank's payment systems are important transfer points for inter-network payments.

At the other end of the spectrum are a number of countries in which the initiative is left primarily to the private sector. In the United Kingdom, for example, the Bank of England's role consists in making accounts available under certain conditions for settlement purposes, while payment processing is carried out mainly by the private sector. In Slovenia the central bank does not provide interbank clearing facilities. As the central bank does not operate a special clearing house for interbank payments, these facilities are provided by commercial banks.

6.4 Central Bank Roles in Transitional Economies

Changes in payment systems since the late 1970s, globalisation and growth in both the value and volume of transactions have not been identical in all countries. Typically, analyses of these issues are made from the viewpoint of the industrial countries in which sophisticated payment systems already exist. But countries that have just started to introduce economic reforms and to rebuild their payment systems are also usually interested in basic payment system issues.

The aim of this section is to analyse the role that central banks can play in payment systems in some transitional countries. Although issues are illustrated using Poland as an example, the situation in most other transitional countries is similar. While not all the experiences of these countries will be relevant for other countries that are currently developing their payment systems, many of the more important problems appear to be.

The political, economic and financial changes in the 1990s in countries such as China, Poland, Russia and Tanzania have placed significant strains on their payment systems. At the outset of their payment system reforms, all these countries possessed government-owned monobanking systems. Initially, there was only one bank (the central bank) in China and Russia. In addition to the central bank, some government-owned and government-controlled banks providing agriculture credits, raising domestic saving and facilitating foreign trade transactions existed in Poland and Tanzania. However, there was deliberately no competition between these banks.

The role of the central banks in these countries at this stage of development was very different from the role of central banks in market-based economies. Central banks were responsible for issuing money, for fulfilling the state budget, for maintaining accounts of enterprises and households, and for providing settlement services and credits to enterprises. In Russia, the central bank was also involved in collecting taxes. Another major purpose of the central bank was to monitor the state plan. This plan determined centrally all the production and distribution decisions that are made independently by individual firms and households in a market economy. Typically, public saving was channelled to enterprises requiring credit under the state plan. Credit was automatic and payments were assured through the monobanking system.

Until the start of the reforms in China, Poland and Russia, payment systems were characterised by a clear separation of cash and noncash circuits. The cash circuit was for households and the noncash circuit for enterprises—usually state-owned firms that were obliged to use a bank account. The main noncash payment instruments consisted of the credit transfer (credit instrument initiated by the payer) and the payment demand order (a debit instrument initiated by the payee following shipment of goods). The central bank debited the payer's bank immediately after receiving a credit transfer order but credited the payee's bank with a lag. In the case of a debit instrument, the payee's bank was credited before the payer's bank was debited.

In both cases this resulted in payment system float that either decreased commercial bank reserves at the central bank (credit float) or increased commercial bank reserves (debit float). Erratic procedures and delays in processing payments produced large and variable float. In China, Poland and Russia, payment clearing relied on the physical transport (by postal services) of detailed paper documentation for each transaction. Because of the country size, transport between the initial debit or credit entry and the registration in the books of the other bank involved in the transaction often took several weeks, so creating enormous float in China and Russia.

Another common feature of payment systems in these countries was the decentralisation of commercial banks' current accounts. Every branch of a commercial bank (where commercial banks existed) kept a clearing account with the local branch of the central bank. Moreover, each branch had to maintain its individual reserve requirements. Reserves were maintained in separate accounts that could not be used for payment purposes. Banks often had large surpluses of funds in some branches and at the same time were paying a penalty for reserve shortfalls in other branches.

The reform of the banking sectors in these countries has required large changes in the arrangements outlined above. This has involved redefining the operational and regulatory roles of the central bank, introducing appropriate accounting procedures and creating new payment systems. Although the starting points in such countries as China, Poland and Russia were similar, the next section examines the Polish reforms in more detail.

6.5 The Case of Poland

In 1990 Poland adopted an adjustment programme, known as the Balcerowicz Plan, to reduce inflation and liberalise the economy. In parallel with the economic reform, both the National Bank of Poland (NBP) and the financial sector required reform. Under the new Banking Law of 1989 that ended the monobanking system, the NBP became the central bank and its commercial banking functions were spun off into nine state-owned commercial banks. There followed very rapid development of the banking sector—by 1992 some 100 private banks had been established.

One aspect of the reform of this young banking system was the creation of a new payment system. The objectives were to accelerate settlement, to reduce risk and to increase the efficiency of monetary policy. Although these aims were expressed at the start of the economic reform process, serious discussions about payment system risk

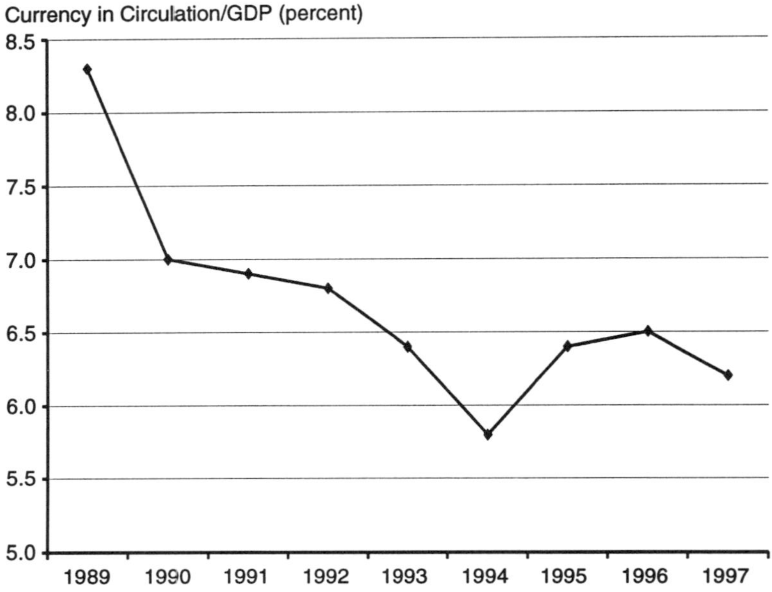

Figure 6.1. The Ratio of Currency in Circulation to Gross Domestic Product in Poland, 1989–1997

and inefficiencies of the existing payment system, e.g., large and volatile float, unreliable timing and execution of payment orders, inefficiencies caused by the decentralisation of bank funds, problems with operating monetary policy, etc., started only in 1991 after two large payment frauds.

At that time there was a distinction between the socialised and private sectors. State-owned enterprises were obliged to use bank accounts and to make noncash payments. Banks served households mainly as savings depositories; banks did not provide households with any payment services. As a result, there was still a noncash circuit for payments in the socialised sector and a cash circuit for payments of the private sector and households. Because of high inflation and demands for cash, the President of the NBP prohibited the use of cash for payments exceeding a certain value between economic units. Figure 6.1 shows the consequent decline in the currency/GDP ratio from 1989 to 1994.

At the beginning of the banking reform, most noncash payments were executed within the NBP. The NBP operated through independent branches serving their customers and keeping their own books. Each

NBP branch maintained accounts for all other branches. Book entries on these accounts were controlled by a centralised computer system working with data delivered by branches. Payment documents were sent directly from branch to branch by standard postal services, which sometimes took several days.

Until 1992, commercial bank branches maintained their current accounts at 49 regional branches of the NBP. Banks were obliged to transfer funds between their branches and to maintain reserve balance accounts in each branch. For credit transfers, the originating bank debited the customers' accounts and then sent a list of credit transfers to the regional NBP branch, which debited the originating bank and credited an interbank clearing account with the NBP. After a delay of some days, the branches of other banks received information on these credit transfers and sent their lists to their regional NBP branch. This NBP branch credited the receiving banks' current accounts and debited the interbank clearing account.

Credit transfers were the most popular payment instruments, so the NBP usually had a credit float on its books. Commercial banks had no incentive to speed up the process because they benefited from delaying transmission of the payment lists. Hence, the banks were able to debit customers' accounts before their own accounts were debited by the NBP.

The transition to a two-tier system transformed what had been an internal float between branches of the central bank into a float involving different institutions. Technical difficulties and the lack of profit orientation on the part of newly created state-owned commercial banks produced long delays in executing transactions. Furthermore, the volume of transactions increased dramatically because of the creation of many new private enterprises. Payment system regulations failed to penalise such delays in processing.

Positive float, i.e., an excess of gross debit transfers over gross credit transfers, was less frequent than negative float.[2] This float was large—reaching 10 per cent of reserve money in early 1990—and variable.[3] Difficulties in predicting movements in float complicated monetary management in Poland. It was almost impossible to set the

---

[2]Negative float implies that credit float exceeds debit float, a situation one would anticipate in a system where credit transfers predominate over debit transfers.

[3]Tomás Baliño, Juhi Dhawan and Venkataraman Sundararajan (1994, Figure 6, p. 403) compare float as a percentage of reserve money in Poland and the United States, 1990–1992. Float in Poland ranges from 2 to 10 percent of reserve money while float in the United States ranges from 0.05 to 0.5 percent of reserve money.

size or even the direction of appropriate monetary operations because it was impossible to forecast demand for bank reserves, money and credit aggregates.

Although net float was negative, i.e., credit float exceeded debit float, both the commercial banks and the NBP assumed significant credit risk, especially when banks granted immediate credit to the payee from debit transfers; the payer was debited only after its bank received the cheque. In 1991 a large-scale cheque-kiting scam was uncovered. A private holding company ART–B used guaranteed cheques to finance its activity. This one company increased the value of debit float to such an extent that net float in the banking system became positive. When the NBP introduced new rules on cheques, which forced banks to receive telecommunication confirmations of balances on payers' accounts before crediting payees, banks realised that there was no money in ART–B's account. The company failed, as did one of commercial banks that had guaranteed the cheques.

After the ART–B case, implementation of new arrangements became a matter of urgency. In these circumstances the role of the central bank was crucial and the NBP implemented the following measures:

- Consolidated banks' clearing accounts into a single account per bank (April 1991 to September 1992). The consolidation of clearing accounts has reduced banks' need for excess reserves, has facilitated banks' liquidity management and has fostered the development of the money market.

- Implemented a communication infrastructure providing a network between banks.

- Introduced the "no overdrafts" rule. This means that banks' payment orders are executed only if there are sufficient funds in the payer's current account. Some rules concerning cheques (notification by telex) that decreased debit float from almost 11 per cent of reserve money in June 1991 to about 2.6 per cent in October 1991 were also introduced. However, these new rules did not change the clearing and settlement mechanism (through branches of NBP) that has deterred almost completely the use of cheques in Poland. Float continued but became negative (banks credited the central bank).

- Prepared the rules for the National Clearing House (NCH). The NCH started its activity in April 1993. The NCH operates two clearing systems: paper based and electronic. At the same time, current accounts of the NCH members were moved to the NBP head office.

- Established a new department (Interbank Settlements Department) responsible for managing the new settlement system and overseeing the interbank payment system.
- Established an RTGS system (SORBNET) operated by the Interbank Settlement Department.
- Implemented an automated book-entry securities system for dematerialised treasury bills issued by the Ministry of Finance. Transactions in the treasury bill market are conducted on a delivery versus payment (DVP) basis.

Theoretically, the introduction of the new payment system in April 1993 should have accelerated the processing of payment instructions and decreased float in the banking system. Figure 6.2 shows that there was indeed a significant decrease in the positive float on the central bank's books. However, Figure 6.3 shows that this was matched by a large increase in the commercial banks' positive float against their customers. This implied that the implementation of the new, much more effective, system shifted float from the central bank to the commercial banks. It also shows that commercial banks did not use the new possibilities to speed up the transfer of funds between their clients. One of the reasons for such behaviour was the lack of competition in the banking sector. Nevertheless, these funds did enable banks to create an interbank money market that became the main source of liquidity. Naturally, this had some consequences for the policy of the central bank concerning liquidity in the RTGS system. The introduction of an RTGS system increases the demand for reserves that central banks may wish to satisfy by creating additional liquidity, e.g., through intraday credit facilities.

In Poland the policy of the central bank is to decrease bank liquidity because banks are able to use required reserves, which are high in Poland compared with other European countries, for settlement purposes. Hence, reserves and the interbank money market are the main sources of liquidity. Figure 6.4 presents the ratio of excess reserves to the sum of excess and compulsory current account reserves held by the commercial banks at the NBP. It indicates that Polish banks hold considerable levels of excess reserves that appear to constitute expensive liquidity for payment purposes.

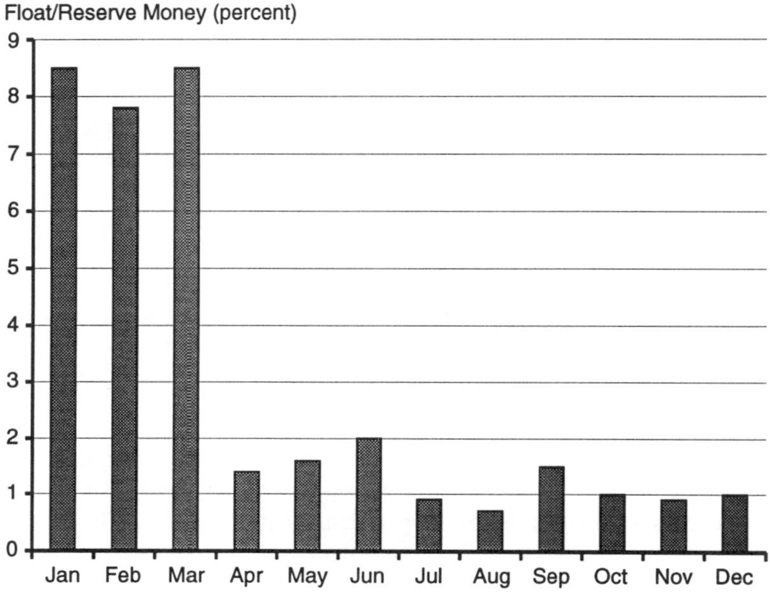

Figure 6.2. Net Float in the National Bank of Poland, 1993

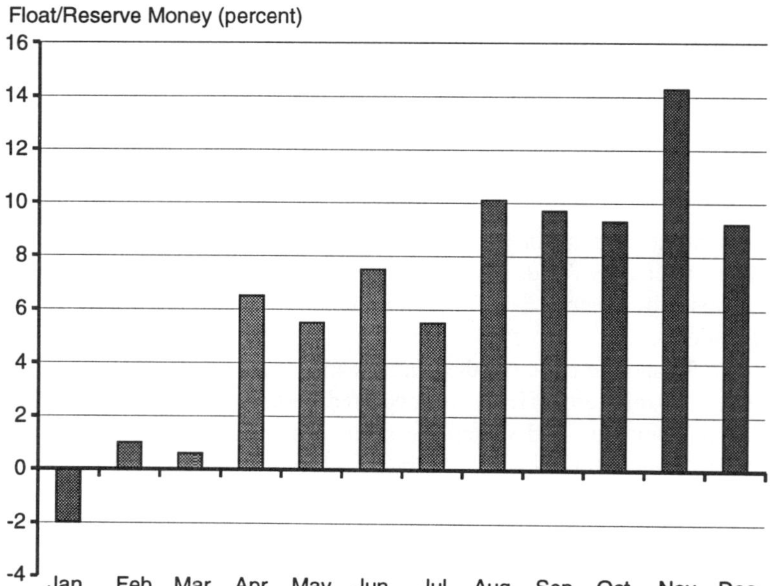

Figure 6.3. Net Float in Polish Commercial Banks, 1993

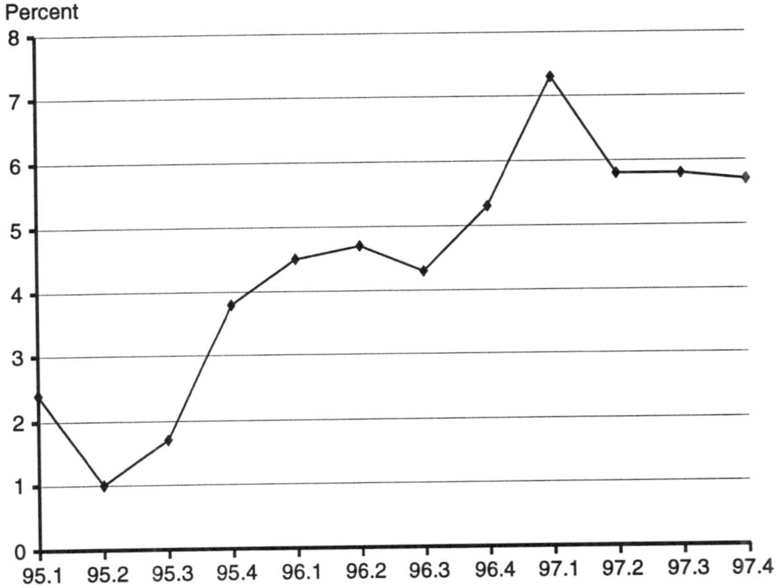

Figure 6.4. Excess Reserves in the Polish Banking System (as percent of banks' current accounts at the National Bank of Poland)

The implementation of these measures took some years. When the NBP started to design a new payment system, there were not enough internal resources and experience to develop a modern payment system quickly. Development of the Polish payment system has been accomplished step by step. The first step was to dismantle the old system and to establish paper-based clearing-house and gross settlement systems. The second step was to introduce electronic systems both through the NCH and the NBP (the SORBNET RTGS system).

6.6 Some Specific Payment Issues in Russia and China

In the early 1990s, rapid economic change in Russia created serious difficulties for its payment system. Each of Russia's 80 regions possesses a central bank branch that plays a key role in the complex process of making inter-regional payments, particularly in the light of the considerable geographical dispersion of enterprises.

As in Poland, a large number of commercial banks were established at the beginning of Russia's economic reforms. At that time, the settlement system was very simple because most banks did not have inter-regional branch networks; they operated in only one region. All payments were cleared directly between banks but often took several weeks because of slow postal services.

One of the first changes introduced by Central Bank of Russia (CBR) was the establishment of Cash and Settlement Centres (CSCs). These enabled all branches of commercial banks to hold their accounts at CSCs. To execute payment orders, banks send them (in paper form) to their CSC. The CSC debits the account of the payer's bank and sends the package through the central bank delivery system to the CSC of the payee's bank. After that, the account of the payee's bank is credited and the package is transferred to this bank. The time of delivery between two CSCs is limited to five days.

The next step to be taken will be the introduction of an RTGS system. The CBR has decided to establish a fully centralised system for all branches of the central bank and for all it clients, i.e., commercial banks and clearing houses, of which there are several.[4] Eventually accounts of all the CBR's clients will be transferred from CSCs to a Federal Settlement Centre, which will then be responsible for all payments. Despite these reforms, many problems specific to Russia still need to be addressed. The most important of these problems are:

- Not all of clients can prepare documents in electronic form. Indeed, there are no commercial banks in some regions, so the CBR maintains personal accounts for people living in such places.
- The lack of an interbank communication system; some places can be reached only by helicopter.
- There are 11 time zones in Russia and so the future RTGS system will operate from 4.00 a.m. to 8.00 p.m.
- Because of the size of the country developing and maintaining terrestrial lines would be very costly, if not impossible. This is why the new system will use a very small aperture terminal (VSAT) network; the first satellite fully owned by the CBR was launched in November 1997.

Until 1979 there was a monobanking system in China. Between 1979 and 1984 this system was replaced by four specialised banks. In

[4]However, clearing houses do not play an important role in the Russian payment system.

1983, the People's Bank of China (PBC) became a central bank. As in Poland and Russia, the PBC provided settlement accounts for specialised banks and in addition operated 2,000 Local Clearing Houses. All these systems were paper-based and usually operated manually. In the period between 1985 and 1993 new regional, national banks and nonbank financial institutions were established. The paper-based system was very slow and float reached astronomical levels. In 1989 the PBC introduced its first electronic interbank payment system, while four major banks introduced their own intrabank electronic systems.

6.7 Conclusion

For transitional economies we draw the following conclusions from the material presented in this chapter:

1. There are some similarities in transitional economies' starting points:

   - monobank or state-owned banking systems;
   - cash-based economies;
   - technologically and institutionally underdeveloped payment systems;
   - insufficient recognition of the importance of the time value of money and of opportunity costs in general;
   - absence of competition;
   - insensitivity to customer needs.

2. Initial conditions and changes introduced on a step-by-step basis to date suggest that central banks in transitional economies probably assume, and need to assume, more responsibilities than central banks in market economies in leading and coordinating payment system reforms. The commercial banks were not strong enough to develop new payment systems on their own. Resources and skilled personnel were lacking, as was experience in the young private sector. The costs of the reform were too high for new small banks. Furthermore, the central bank was able to receive and coordinate financial help and technical assistance from other central banks and international institutions. Perhaps as a consequence, the similarities in the sequencing of banking system reforms in transitional economies have been quite striking.

3. Because of the lack of resources, the shortages of skilled personnel and the lack of experience in the private sector, the central bank is forced to play important roles in all aspects of payment system design and development. Consequently, central banks in transitional economies typically assume prominent operational roles.

4. Emerging economies can adapt successful systems and practices from the industrial countries to suit their own needs. These countries can learn from the experiences of as well as the mistakes made in industrial countries. Furthermore, they can choose design options for modernising their payment systems that were not available in the past to industrial countries.

5. Optimal sequencing of payment system development may be similar, e.g., accounts in branches of central bank, consolidation of these accounts, paper-based systems and then RTGS adoption, across transitional economies. Many countries chose an evolutionary approach and did not leapfrog to the latest technology. Users and suppliers in industrial countries possess experience with noncash payment systems and infrastructures that support noncash payments. Such experience did not and still does not exist in many transitional and developing countries. Rapid change in payment systems may not be practical from financial, institutional or human resource standpoints. Initial efforts should be implementable and practical. The critical payment design issue is to identify the most important payment applications and develop a system that can be easily installed and used in commercial and central banks.

6. Many transitional countries suffer legal deficiencies, e.g., physical authentication by means of signature is or was the only legally acceptable method of authenticating a payment.

7. In market economies, banks have profit incentives to develop payment services that meet the needs of their customers. So market forces influence the development of payment services. In transitional economies, the profit incentive is still in its infancy.

One consequence is that there is little customer pressure for improved payment services.[5]

8. Central and commercial banks provide and promote different types of payment services in transitional economies because individuals still rely heavily on cash. This implies that considerable potential exists for commercial banks to expand their markets by developing the banking habit.

9. In countries such as China and Russia, where central bank operations are spread over vast distances and where there tends to be a high degree of regional autonomy, progress with payment system reforms has had to focus on developing strong centralised control. In the absence of such severe internal management problems, the central banks in Poland and Tanzania have been able to focus on cooperating with the commercial banks to promote reforms in their payment systems.

10. Changes in the timing of debits and credits influencing the size and variability of float have caused serious problems for monetary control in the transitional economies.

11. Data for transitional countries are still inadequate. Because of insufficient data on the share of cash payments, velocity and float, large discrete changes in payment system arrangements in transitional and developing countries necessitate the close attention of central banks to the linkages between payment systems and monetary policy. The next chapter addresses these links in some detail.

[5]The apposite expression used in Eastern Europe is: "It is easier to get people out of communism than communism out of people."

Chapter 7

Some Links between Payment Systems, Monetary Policy, Fixed Exchange Rates and Financial Stability

7.1 Introduction

BECAUSE THEY INVOLVE TRANSFERRING MONEY between payers and payees, payment systems constitute the link between money and economic activity. The efficiency with which money is used is largely determined by the efficiency of the payment system. On the one hand, monetary policy cannot be implemented in the absence of a payment system, nor can it be implemented *efficiently* without an *efficient* payment system. On the other hand, the monetary policy framework may itself affect the efficiency of a country's payment system. So the next section considers the relationship between payment systems and monetary policy.

A country's exchange rate regime can affect the payment process when it comes under stress. A drain of liquidity during a speculative attack against a fixed or managed exchange rate necessarily affects the payment system adversely. In contrast to the link between payment systems and monetary policy, section 7.3 suggests that there are no channels through which payment arrangements can themselves affect the exchange rate regime.

Payment systems are also linked to financial stability because financial instability can be transmitted through the payment system at a speed limited only by the speed of the payment system itself. Conversely, financial instability impinges on the payment system when a participant fails to settle a payment. So section 7.4 examines the links between payment systems and financial stability. Both the monetary policy and the financial stability links provide further grounds for central bank oversight, if not active involvement, in a country's payment system.

7.2 Payment System Linkages with Monetary Policy

This section concentrates on the payment system as a tool for day-to-day monetary policy implementation. The shift in monetary policy emphasis from direct controls on interest rates and credit to indirect management of commercial banks' reserves/liquidity through open market operations has served to emphasise the critical importance of reliable and efficient same-day payment and settlement arrangements. Such arrangements will increase the effectiveness of central banks' indirect monetary management and liquidity adjustment techniques in three ways:

- They contribute towards a stable demand for reserves by the banks.
- They enable the authorities to measure accurately the impact on the supply of reserves of government receipts/spending and foreign exchange intervention.
- They facilitate the development of deep and liquid interbank and money markets.

For example, an automated same-day payment system can help the monetary authority implement a genuinely nationwide monetary policy by providing the mechanism whereby arbitrage activity equalises interest rates across different regions/centres of activity. This has been a major objective of the project to develop a nationwide electronic large-value payment system in China and it is one of the key purposes for the TARGET euro payment system that is to operate in the European Monetary Union (EMU) area from 4 January 1999.

Managing commercial bank liquidity can also be examined in terms of payment float that creates windfall gains or costs to those involved in the payment process arising when the accounting entries for the two sides of a payment are not posted simultaneously. As discussed in the previous chapter, large and variable float is associated with inefficient payment and settlement arrangements. It is exacerbated by highly decentralised accounting structures in which individual commercial banks have local settlement accounts at regional branches of the central bank. When time lags between the original debiting of a paying bank's local settlement account and the eventual crediting of the receiving bank's local settlement account are long and variable, the task of monitoring the overall size of and influences on the banking system's liquidity becomes very difficult. Because of this uncertainty, the banks themselves may hold large excess balances on their settlement accounts and the central bank may feel obliged to offer liberal access to late overnight lending. Both hinder the development of money market instruments and of interbank markets.

Large and variable payment float has been a particularly serious problem for transitional economies and a factor slowing the development of indirect monetary management techniques (Baliño, Dhawan and Sundararajan 1994, pp. 385–386). Following the change from monobanking to two-tier banking, the new and hastily implemented payment arrangements were initially, and unsurprisingly, not very efficient: inadequate rules, underdeveloped technology and a highly decentralised structure.[1] Lack of payment rules and competition produced substantial lengthening of payment cycles, i.e., increased delays, when the central bank attempted to tighten monetary policy (Baliño, Dhawan and Sundararajan 1994, p. 387).

Even when payment float is not an issue because it is either stable or minimal, a major structural change in payment system procedures may still have a significant short-term effect on monetary policy. Switzerland's introduction of an RTGS system (SIC) in June 1987 combined with the reduction in reserve requirements in January 1988 provides an interesting illustration. Because the Swiss National Bank (SNB) was *not* providing any additional intraday liquidity as part of the SIC service (in the form of intraday overdrafts or repos), Swiss commercial banks took steps to improve their own intraday liquidity management (e.g., by more carefully scheduling customer payments through the day), effectively reducing their overall demand for reserves. This behavioural change was not evident to the SNB at the time and was not factored into the reserve requirement reduction that followed a little later. The result

[1] See section 6.5 for a detailed account of the experiences of the National Bank of Poland in this area.

was that, for a period, the SNB's monetary policy was more lax than had been intended.[2]

Conversely, and more generally, the precise monetary management regime that the authorities have adopted may influence the type of payment system that the banks wish to develop, principally through the effect on the opportunity cost of central bank money. So where there are high reserve requirements, where such reserve balances can be used to settle payments within the day, and where perhaps interest is paid on overnight balances at the central bank, the commercial banks' enthusiasm for a "liquidity expensive" RTGS system *vis-à-vis* a "liquidity cheap" multilateral net end-of-day settlement system is likely to rise.

No discussion of payment system/monetary policy linkages is complete without some mention of the possibility of a spillover of intraday payment system credit into overnight credit, and the potential effect of such an event on overall monetary conditions. Among central bankers it is generally accepted that (a) explicit provision of secured intraday credit to RTGS systems is a "good thing" on payment system efficiency grounds, and (b) despite the potential for spillover, central banks can introduce safeguards such that, on the rare occasions when it does occur, the effect is negligible. In other words, intraday and overnight/interday markets can be effectively segmented by, for example, imposing an early cut-off time for customer payments (so that banks can use the last period before the payment system closes to square their positions) and a penal regime for any "spillover" lending. Hence, monetary policy can still operate effectively in the context of end-of-day balances and overnight (or longer) interest rates (Dale and Rossi 1996).

The spillover issue has featured prominently in discussions about the terms on which the United Kingdom and the other "out" countries not adopting the euro from 4 January 1999 can connect to the TARGET euro payment system. The TARGET system has been designed with the twin objectives of supporting the single monetary policy in the euro area and of providing a sound and efficient same-day payment mechanism across the whole European Union. It will essentially be made up of interlinked national RTGS systems and so its efficiency relies on the provision of sufficient intraday credit. Despite the conclusions reached in the previous paragraph, however, there has been a reluctance on the part of a number of the "in" countries to extend intraday euro credit to "out" countries like the United Kingdom because of a perceived

[2] This happened only because at the time the SNB was pursuing a monetary base target.

risk of such credit spilling over into overnight credit and so affecting monetary conditions in the EMU area. Fortunately, the EU central banks have arrived at a practical solution to this issue which both supports the TARGET system's need for adequate intraday credit and avoids the perceived risks to the EMU area's monetary policy stance.

7.3 Payment Systems and Fixed Exchange Rates

The spillover question appears to be most serious when the authorities are following a fixed/managed exchange rate policy. Thus, in a situation of heavy speculative selling of the domestic currency, banks may be unable to pay the central bank or, in an RTGS system to repay intraday credit, at the end-of-day settlement. Should the central bank accommodate this spillover and provide the overnight funds or take a hard line with the banks? In recent times, both Hong Kong and Mexico have had to face this difficult choice.

Provision of intraday liquidity for payment purposes raises no particular problems for countries with floating exchange rates. Since the central bank conducts no foreign exchange operations under a floating exchange rate system, the form of payment system and the foreign exchange settlement arrangements are irrelevant. At present, the standard settlement arrangements for foreign exchange transactions are two days after the transaction, i.e., $t + 2$. In this case, whether or not the payment system is DNS or RTGS or whether or not the central bank provides intraday liquidity is also irrelevant. No liquidity is needed until settlement day.

In the more unusual case of same-day foreign exchange settlement, banks might be tempted to use intraday liquidity for speculative purposes were they expecting to replace it before the end of day through foreign exchange sales to the central bank.

Managing the exchange rate obliges the central bank to buy and sell foreign exchange at the managed price. This process necessarily alters the total amount of reserve money. In this case, therefore, there can be no presumption that banks will be able to repay intraday credit to the central bank simply by reallocating a fixed amount of reserve money through the interbank market at the end of each day. If the central bank has sold foreign exchange under same-day settlement, there is less reserve money available at the end of the day than there was at the beginning of the day.

Indeed, commercial banks could produce just such a situation were they all to buy foreign exchange with their intraday credit from the central bank or, of course, with any other reserve money balances. Even if the banks were aware that liquidity would be unavailable to repay intraday loans to the central bank in the evening, they would be undeterred from their speculative acquisition of foreign exchange provided they could obtain overnight credit from the central bank at a preannounced rate of interest which was not sufficiently high to offset the expected currency gain.

In essence, the situation differs only in its time dimension when we consider the more common practice of DNS with a two-day delay in foreign exchange settlement. Indeed, the latter situation could be even more difficult because banks are able to agree spot foreign exchange purchases without actually possessing the reserves with which to settle. These are needed only two days later. So speculation in spot foreign exchange purchases could exceed the existing total of good funds, something that would be impossible in a same-day settlement environment.

Central banks responsible for managing their exchange rates need contingency plans to defend their currencies against speculative attack. Defence is effectively impossible if commercial banks can borrow unlimited amounts of the domestic currency at the normal preannounced rate of interest and available collateral far exceeds the foreign exchange reserves available to the central bank. So one deterrent would be to auction collateral in the event that intraday credit was unpaid. In such case, however, the shortage of reserve money would ensure that such securities could be sold—if they could be sold at all—only at massive discounts. Domestic interest rates could rise so high that the auction yielded insufficient funds to effect repayment.

While haircuts may be devised to minimise this possibility, flexibility is unlikely to be sufficient in the face of a speculative attack. Under these conditions, the values of even short-term securities can fall dramatically. Therefore, foreign assets constitute the ultimate collateral against intraday credit in managed exchange rate regimes. This is approximately the Hong Kong Monetary Authority's practice of requiring Exchange Fund bonds, which are backed 100 percent by foreign reserves, as collateral for intraday credit. Any central bank obliged to manage the country's exchange rate could offer intraday repos only against foreign exchange-denominated assets to avoid the risk of plunging values of domestic collateral.

The battle against a speculative attack on the domestic currency is won when the commercial banks start selling foreign exchange to the central bank because of the domestic liquidity shortage. The only credible scheme to defend the exchange rate is one whereby speculators face the prospects of losing money. It is difficult to envisage any feasible alternative to making overnight central bank credit exorbitantly expensive at some limit. Speculative attacks on a currency reduce available liquidity, unless the central bank accommodates the shortfall. One cannot deny that vigorous currency defence will strain the payment process. That is because liquidity provided for payment—RTGS or DNS—or for any other purpose can and will be used in any speculative attack unless there is a clearly announced policy of penalising such action so severely that banks stand to make considerable losses if the speculative attack fails. The same caveat applies to reserve averaging under a system of required reserves: a speculative attack can draw down reserves early during the averaging period at no cost, provided the attack succeeds before the end of reserve maintenance period.

In the case of any major currency, central bank attempts to deter speculative attacks by requiring cash in advance for foreign exchange payments, etc., cannot succeed because markets cannot be segmented. Alternative payment systems and alternative markets can always be used. If the RTGS system is unsatisfactory for foreign exchange transactions, a DNS system will be used. If foreign exchange markets in one country are impeded, speculators will use markets in other countries. A fixed exchange rate requires the central bank to provide foreign exchange whenever and wherever it is demanded at the fixed price. Otherwise, the exchange rate will not be fixed. The only alternative is the reimposition of comprehensive foreign exchange controls. The difficulty with this is that it requires an army of foreign exchange controllers to be conjured immediately into existence.

7.4 Payment System Linkages with Financial Stability and Surveillance

Technological advances in recent years have meant that ever-larger payment flows are being processed with ever-increasing speed. Given any understanding of the payment system's fundamental role in a developed market economy's financial infrastructure, therefore, the existence of important linkages between payment systems and financial stability are not difficult to visualise.

In payment systems, one bank's payment is another bank's liquidity. A failure to transfer funds for whatever reason could lead to similar failures by other system participants who were relying on those payments. Even those not directly involved with the bank experiencing the original failure may be affected. Failure to meet payment obligations will lead quickly to loss of confidence and reappraisals of credit-worthiness, both among the community of payment system banks and more widely among the financial market participants. They are the banks' customers who in turn may find their payment obligations unfulfilled. This effect may be especially marked if confidence in particular institutions or markets is already fragile or shaken.

Payment systems not only represent a potential source of systemic disturbance in themselves but also have the potential to transmit financial shocks and problems from their initial source to other parts of the financial system—and even to magnify them. So market rumours about one bank's credit-worthiness could encourage other banks to delay sending payments to it until they received expected payments in advance. Alternatively, were the payment system in question a net settlement arrangement with intraday limits between members, then the "rumoured" bank could find its intraday limits cut and its ability to send and receive payments reduced. In both cases, the risk of gridlock and hence systemic disruption has been increased.

Payment system linkages with financial stability do not respect national frontiers. Payment systems—even if notionally operating within a single country—are increasingly international in nature. Participation in payment systems by branches of foreign banks is commonplace. It is also now technically possible to "remote access" a payment system, i.e., to be a direct participant and have the necessary settlement account at the central bank without actually having a physical banking presence in the country concerned. But more fundamentally, a high proportion of payments processed through "domestic" payment systems relate to transactions between parties in third countries that utilise the worldwide correspondent banking network to fulfil their payment obligations. The largest and most obvious instance of this is, of course, the foreign exchange market. And one of the clearest illustrations of the cross-border nature of the linkage remains the Herstatt episode in 1974, when the failure of a relatively small bank in Germany following overtrading in the foreign exchange market led to some quite serious disturbance in the New York-based dollar clearing system (CHIPS) when the Herstatt Bank's dollar obligations were not met.

A particular and interesting instance of the payment system/financial stability linkage is presented when markets use a central counterparty/clearing house for their clearing and risk management arrangements.

Examples here would include the exchange-traded derivatives markets (for example, the London Clearing House clearing for the London International Financial Futures and Options Exchange LIFFE) and foreign exchange clearing by London's Exchange Clearing House Organisation (ECHO). By substituting itself as the counterparty to trades between the market participants, the clearing house aims to provide its members with multilateral offsetting of their originally bilateral exposures and to manage safely the risks that it has assumed. A vital element of this process is the robustness of the clearing house's arrangements for collecting and disbursing funds/financial assets when they are due. Having effectively concentrated the members' exposures onto the clearing house, the implications of a problem—real or rumoured—for that clearing house in meeting its obligations could have serious repercussions for the market concerned.

The most dramatic and high-profile aspect of this payment system/financial stability linkage arises when the central bank has to decide whether or not to act as lender of last resort during a financial crisis. In other words, should the central bank provide the liquidity necessary for a troubled institution to be able to meet its obligations in the payment system during a crisis, or should the central bank, after due consideration, be prepared to accept the consequences of that institution's defaulting on those obligations? The central bank's policy towards and operations as an exceptional lender of last resort are thus closely connected with its policy and operations regarding normal payment system intraday liquidity provision. Certainly, any perception that the central bank views the "spillover" of normal intraday credit into overnight credit as anything other than an exceptional and undesirable event can create conditions in which the lender of last resort "safety net" is abused and moral hazard risk is encouraged.

With this in mind, the tasks of banking supervisors and of central banks as payment system overseer can be viewed as being complementary:

- Banking supervisors must ensure that the banks that are direct participants in the payment system are financially sound. They can also help in the process of ensuring that banks understand properly the particular risks/obligations that they assume as direct participants in their payment system, e.g., the possible loss-sharing obligations in a net settlement system.

- Central banks as payment system overseers can ensure that any such risks/obligations are managed prudently and that, more gen-

> erally, the payment systems are safely operated—either by the central banks themselves running the systems or by imposing rigorous standards on privately operated systems.

The risk management practices adopted in high-value payment systems, whether central bank or privately operated, raise some other interesting issues. On the one hand, moves to collateralise intraday payment system exposures reduce the likely systemic consequences of a payment system participant failure and thereby contribute to a safer and more stable financial environment in which banks and markets can operate. On the other hand, in the event of insolvency, provision of such collateralisation will not be in the direct interests of an individual unsecured depositor, whose interests the banking supervisor is supposed to protect. If it is the central bank that is the holder of this collateral, it could be placed in a particularly invidious position. The central bank can argue that its actions do not change the total loss in the failed bank (caused by extraneous circumstances) but, rather, change the distribution of that loss among creditors while allowing/enabling the payment system as a whole to settle in an orderly way. Undoubtedly, central bank involvement can change the incidence of the loss among creditors.

7.5 Conclusion

The key to ensuring that the linkages between payment systems, monetary policy and financial stability are not disruptive lies in regular contact and information-sharing among those responsible for payment systems, monetary policy and supervision and surveillance of banks and financial markets. This is particularly important when major operational changes are contemplated and when markets and systems are under strain. With close cooperation and communication, there should at least be opportunities to prevent problems developing into crises and to reduce the incidence of "nasty surprises".

Appendix 1

Payment and Settlement Systems Questionnaire

[Please indicate any answers that you wish to be kept confidential or unattributed.]

Please give the name of your national currency:

1. Overview of the payment system

(a) What are the types of systems in use in your country at the moment?

(i) real-time gross settlement (RTGS)

(ii) deferred net settlement

(iii) other (please explain and briefly describe)

(b) Name and description of the system(s), and the number and value of transactions through it (them).

2. Detailed payment information

Please provide annual data (including estimates if accurate data are not available) for the latest calendar year. Transaction values should be given in local currency and US$ equivalent.

(a) Domestic cash payments

(i) volume of transactions

(ii) value of transactions

(b) Domestic noncash payments (analysis by types of instruments)

Instrument	*Volume*	*Percent*	*Value*	*Percent*
Cards (credit and debit)				
Cheques				
Paper credit transfers				
Electronic credit transfers				
Other				

Please describe "other".

3. The role of the central bank

(a) Are the payment systems

(i) owned by the central bank?

(ii) owned by the commercial banks?

(iii) jointly owned?

(b) What is the nature of the central bank's oversight role with respect to the payment system(s)?

(i) formal

(ii) informal

If formal, please summarise the law(s). If informal, please summarise the role.

4. Risk and efficiency issues

(a) What measures are in place to protect the payment systems against settlement risk?

(i) RTGS

- no intraday overdrafts
- overdrafts limits
- collateralised overdrafts

(ii) DNS

- intraday limits (bilateral and/or multilateral)
- collateral requirements
- loss-sharing agreement

Does the central bank, explicitly or implicitly, provide any guarantee in the event of a settlement failure?

Does the central bank incur exposure *vis-à-vis* the commercial banks during the course of payment system operations?

(b) Please give details of the length of the clearing cycles for the various payment systems:

(i) maximum number of days

(ii) minimum number of days

(c) What are the arrangements for the provision for emergency liquidity?

5. Pricing policy

(a) What is the central bank pricing policy as far as payment services are concerned?

(i) free

(ii) subsidised

(iii) full-cost recovery

(iv) target rate of return

(v) other

(b) Please provide a summary (accurate data or estimate) of the commercial banks' pricing policy for payment services.

6. Prerequisites for payment system development

Using the three broad categories below, briefly describe for your country where there are obstacles or deficiencies and how they have been addressed.

(a) Technical infrastructure (telecommunication, computer network)

(b) Legal framework

(c) Maturity of the banking system

7. Payment system strategy

(a) Briefly describe the strategy being adopted by your central bank as regards payment system reform and development. For example, if your country does not have well-developed noncash payment media, is it the intention to follow a traditional/evolutionary approach or to "leapfrog" to the latest technology?

(b) Describe the involvement of the commercial banks in the strategy.

8. Any other problems not previously mentioned

(a) In the past

(b) Now

9. Payment system and monetary policy implementation and transmission

Briefly record your observations on how changes in payment system operations have affected monetary policy implementation and transmission.

10. Commercial bank reserves

(a) If there are any reserve requirements, please give the ratio(s).

(b) Explain the details of the requirements (maintenance period, averaging, etc.).

(c) Do commercial banks hold substantial voluntary (free) reserves? If yes, please indicate the average and the reason(s).

(d) Are required reserves held in a separate account at the central bank?

(e) Does the central bank pay interest on this account? If yes, please give the percentage.

(f) Please give any measure of the volatility of the voluntary reserves, where available.

(g) Can required reserves be used for intraday payment purposes?

Thank you very much for your assistance.

Appendix 2

Deferred Net Settlement Systems

Country	*Exists*	*Comments*
Australia	Yes	Bank Interchange and Transfer System (BITS), Austraclear and SWIFT Payment Delivery System (PDS) together with small-value clearing systems
Austria	No	
Belgium	Yes	For retail payments
Canada	Yes	Currently Automated Clearing Settlement System (ACSS) system; LVTS for large-value payments to be introduced in early 1999
Finland	Yes	Banks' On-line Express Transfer and Cheque System (POPS) together with a separate DNS system for retail payments
France	Yes	Système Net Protégé (SNP)
Germany	No	Euro Access Frankfurt (EAF) is a hybrid system
Greece	Yes	Athens Clearing Office (ACO) is a multilateral paper-based net settlement system for large-value transactions; a separate DNS system exists for retail payments
Hong Kong	Yes	Two retail clearing systems
Iceland	Yes	Multilateral net clearing system for both interbank and retail transactions
Italy	Yes	Primarily retail payments
Netherlands	Yes	Primarily retail payments
New Zealand	Yes	Austraclear
Norway	Yes	Retail and medium-size payments
Portugal	Yes	Retail payments only
Singapore	Yes	System for Handling Interbank Funds Transfers (SHIFT)
Spain	Yes	Servicio Español de Pagos Interbancarios (SEPI) together with a national electronic clearing system for retail transactions
Sweden	No	
Switzerland	No	
United Kingdom	Yes	Three separate clearing systems for retail transactions
United States	Yes	Clearing House Interbank Payment System (CHIPS) together with numerous DNS systems—cheque clearing houses and automated clearing houses (ACHs)—for retail transactions

Deferred Net Settlement Systems (Continued)

Country	*Exists*	*Comments*
Armenia	Yes	Paper-based credit transfers mainly for low-value payments; payment orders are presented in batches at one of the two daily clearing sessions
Belarus	Yes	Belarus Interbank Settlement Center (BISC)
Bulgaria	No	Banking Integrated System for Electronic Transfers (BISERA) is a deferred *gross* system
China	Yes	Local clearing houses that are owned and operated by the central bank together with a nationwide Electronic Interbank System (EIS)
Czech Republic	No	
Hungary	No	Interbank Giro System (IGS) is a deferred *gross* system
Latvia	Yes	Mainly for corporate and retail payments together with a paper-based deferred *gross* system
Poland	Yes	SYBIR and ELIXIR
Russia	Yes	But very limited (six licensed clearing houses for small-value payments); traditional *gross* settlements are effected through central bank's network of cash settlement centres
Slovakia	No	Slovak Interbank Payment System (SIPS) is a deferred *gross* system; all interbank payments are processed electronically through Slovak National Clearing Centre (SNCC)
Slovenia	No	Deferred *gross* settlement across accounts at the Agency for Payments
Tanzania	Yes	Multilateral and bilateral settlement
Vietnam	Yes	Decentralised clearing centres in central bank branches
Bahrain	No	
Barbados	Yes	
Bermuda	Yes	Bermuda Interbank Net Settlement System
Botswana	Yes	
Brazil	Yes	Multilateral Clearing System for Cheques and Remittance Documents (COMPE) clears cheques and electronic interbank credit transfers
Colombia	Yes	Large-value cheque clearing with a separate clearing for plastic card transactions
Cyprus	Yes	Most value in credit transfer (paper and electronic) and cheque clearings
Eastern Caribbean	Yes	For intra-island cheques (multilateral net) and inter-island cheques (bilateral net) together with a deferred *gross* system for interbank payments
Egypt	Yes	
Fiji	Yes	Manual cheque clearing
Guyana	Yes	Multilateral and bilateral cheque-clearing systems
Jordan	Yes	Semi-automatic clearing system

Deferred Net Settlement Systems (Continued)

Country	*Exists*	*Comments*
Kenya	Yes	Bankers' Clearing System mainly processes cheques
Korea	Yes	For retail payments
Kuwait	Yes	Only for plastic card settlement; cheques and interbank credits are settled on a deferred *gross* basis
Lebanon	No	Deferred *gross* settlement
Malawi	Yes	Clearing occurs twice a day and finality of transactions is provided at end of day
Malaysia	Yes	Electronic Funds and Securities Transfer System (SPEEDS) together with automated cheque clearing system
Malta	Yes	For small-value payments (including cheques)
Mauritius	Yes	Port Louis Clearing House
Mexico	Yes	Three systems for retail payments
Morocco	Yes	Together with a deferred *gross* settlement system
Mozambique	No	
Namibia	Yes	Manual clearing and settlement system
Nigeria	Yes	Nigeria Clearing System and Nigeria Inter-Bank Settlement System (NIBSS)
Pakistan	Yes	Regional clearing houses
Peru	Yes	Cheque clearing houses together with a deferred *gross* settlement system for large-value interbank transactions
Saudi Arabia	Yes	Automated cheque clearing house
South Africa	Yes	Traditionally, multilateral DNS on a next-day basis; the recently launched South African Multiple Option Settlement (SAMOS) system includes a hybrid option with prefunded net settlement
Swaziland	Yes	Mbabane Bankers Clearing Manual System
Tonga	Yes	Interbank cheque clearing system (for large- and small-value payments)
Turkey	Yes	Local small-value cheque clearings
Uganda	Yes	Together with a deferred *gross* settlement system for interbank cheques operating in Kampala
United Arab Emirates	Yes	For cheques and electronic credit transfers
Zambia	Yes	Cheque clearing system (with regional clearing houses) with next-day settlement together with an interbank transfer system using deferred *gross* settlement
Zimbabwe	Yes	Manual paper-based

Appendix 3

Real-Time Gross Settlement Systems

Country	*Exists*	*Comments*
Australia	Yes	Since June 1998, Reserve Bank Information and Transfer System (RITS) has provided the central RTGS platform with SWIFT Y-copy used as the delivery network
Austria	Yes	Austrian Real Time Interbank Settlement (ARTIS)
Belgium	Yes	Electronic Large-Value Interbank Payment System (ELLIPS)
Canada	No	
Finland	Yes	Bank of Finland (BoF) system for interbank payments and payments through central bank's accounts
France	Yes	Transferts Banque de France (TBF) from October 1997
Germany	Yes	Euro Link System (ELS) used mainly by banks for interbank transactions and open-market operations
Greece	Yes	Hellenic Real-time Money transfer Express System (HERMES) from June 1998
Hong Kong	Yes	Clearing House Automated Transfer System (CHATS) from December 1996
Iceland	No	
Italy	Yes	Banca d'Italia Regolamento Lordo (BI-REL) launched in June 1997 (operational since January 1998) settles all interbank large-value payments
Netherlands	Yes	TOP system
New Zealand	Yes	Since March 1998, RTGS system settles large-value wholesale transactions
Norway	Yes	NBO for large-value transfer payments from November 1997
Portugal	Yes	Sistema de Pagamentos de Grandes Transacções (SPGT) for large-value transfers, money market operations, interbank credits over Esc 100 million
Singapore	No	MAS is developing an RTGS system called MAS Electronic Payment System (MEPS)
Spain	Yes	Settlement Service of the Banco de España (SLBE)
Sweden	Yes	Clearing and Interbank System (RIX)
Switzerland	Yes	Swiss Interbank Clearing (SIC)
United Kingdom	Yes	Clearing House Automated Payment System (CHAPS) from April 1996
United States	Yes	FedWire

Real-Time Gross Settlement Systems (Continued)

Country	*Exists*	*Comments*
Armenia	Yes	Paper-based and electronic settlement (BankMail) system used mainly for large-value transactions
Belarus	Yes	Due to be introduced in 1998
Bulgaria	No	
China	No	But a nationwide RTGS system is the key element in the ongoing China National Advanced Payment System (CNAPS) project
Czech Republic	Yes	
Hungary	No	
Latvia	Yes	Electronic Funds Transfer System (EFTS)
Poland	Yes	SORBNET
Russia	No	But nationwide RTGS being developed
Slovakia	No	
Slovenia	No	
Tanzania	No	
Vietnam	No	

Real-Time Gross Settlement Systems (Continued)

Country	*Exists*	*Comments*
Bahrain	Yes	For all types of transactions
Barbados	No	
Bermuda	No	
Botswana	No	
Brazil	No	
Colombia	Yes	Banco de la República Electronic Services (SEBRA) for interbank credit transfers
Cyprus	No	
Eastern Caribbean	No	
Egypt	No	
Fiji	No	
Guyana	No	
Jordan	Yes	Manual paper-based RTGS system
Kenya	No	
Korea	Yes	BoK-wire for large-value payments since December 1994
Kuwait	No	
Lebanon	No	
Malawi	No	
Malaysia	No	
Malta	Yes	For interbank payments
Mauritius	No	
Mexico	Yes	Sistema de Informació a Cuentahabientes (SIAC) and Sistema de Pagos Electrónicos de Uso Ampliado (SPEUA) for large-value payments
Morocco	No	
Mozambique	No	
Namibia	No	
Nigeria	No	
Pakistan	No	
Peru	No	
Saudi Arabia	Yes	Saudi Arabian Riyal Interbank Express (SARIE) for wholesale and bulk interbank payments
South Africa	Yes	SAMOS launched in March 1998 includes an RTGS option
Swaziland	No	
Tonga	No	
Turkey	Yes	Turkish Interbank Clearing System (TIC-RTGS) for both large- and small-value value transactions from 1992
Uganda	No	
United Arab Emirates	No	
Zambia	No	
Zimbabwe	No	

Appendix 4

Central Bank Risk Exposure

Country	*Exists*	*Comments*
Australia	Yes	As a payment system participant, central bank contributes to loss-sharing arrangements
Austria	No	
Belgium	No	Despite the residual risk in foreign exchange operations
Canada	Yes	In ACSS there is no exposure in its capacity as settlement agent but central bank could be exposed in its capacity as participant of the system; in LVTS, central bank provides explicit guarantee (see Appendix 5)
Finland	No	
France	No	
Germany	No	
Greece	No	
Hong Kong	No	
Iceland	Yes	Indirect responsibility of the central bank in case of settlement failure
Italy	No	
Netherlands	No	
New Zealand	No	
Norway	No	
Portugal	No	
Singapore	No	MAS has right to unwind transactions in DNS system in event of settlement failure
Spain	No	
Sweden	No	
Switzerland	No	
United Kingdom	No	
United States	No	Although capped uncollateralised intraday overdrafts are allowed in FedWire for healthy institutions

Central Bank Risk Exposure (Continued)

Country	*Exists*	*Comments*
Armenia	No	
Belarus	n.a.	
Bulgaria	No	
China	Yes	
Czech Republic	No	
Hungary	No	
Latvia	No	Intraday and overnight credits are granted only against collateral
Poland	No	
Russia	No	
Slovakia	No	
Slovenia	No	
Tanzania	Yes	
Vietnam	n.a.	

Central Bank Risk Exposure (Continued)

Country	*Exists*	*Comments*
Bahrain	No	
Barbados	No	
Bermuda	No	
Botswana	Yes	
Brazil	Yes	If settlement problems occur intraday, the central bank would step in and could therefore incur losses
Colombia	No	
Cyprus	n.a.	Considered to be negligible
Eastern Caribbean	Yes	Central bank can be exposed to banks that have failed to cover their outgoing payment position during the day and have unauthorised overnight overdrafts
Egypt	No	
Fiji	No	
Guyana	No	
Jordan	No	
Kenya	No	
Korea	No	
Kuwait	Yes	Central bank incurs risk throughout the business day until the end-of-day transactions have been settled
Lebanon	No	
Malawi	No	
Malaysia	Yes	
Malta	No	
Mauritius	No	
Mexico	Yes	
Morocco	Yes	But reduced because banks must provide a minimum treasury bill portfolio as security
Mozambique	Yes	
Namibia	Yes	
Nigeria	Yes	Exposed when collateral falls short of overdrawn position
Pakistan	Yes	As clearing house participant
Peru	Yes	
Saudi Arabia	No	
South Africa	Yes	Traditionally, the central bank has faced overnight risk; the new SAMOS system removes the risk from the high-value payment system
Swaziland	Yes	
Tonga	No	
Turkey	No	
Uganda	Yes	
United Arab Emirates	Yes	
Zambia	Yes	
Zimbabwe	n.a.	

Appendix 5

Central Bank Settlement Failure Guarantee

Country	*Exists*	*Comments*
Australia	Yes	Implicit guarantee: if bank declared "failed to settle", the loss-sharing arrangement would apply. Reserve Bank of Australia (RBA) may provide temporarily enough funds to allow the daily settlement
Austria	No	
Belgium	No	
Canada	Yes	ACSS carries no guarantee but central bank guarantees explicitly that settlement will take place under the LVTS system when two or more participants fail simultaneously
Finland	No	
France	No	
Germany	No	
Greece	No	
Hong Kong	No	
Iceland	Yes	Central bank carries indirect responsibility in the event of a settlement failure
Italy	No	
Netherlands	No	
New Zealand	No	
Norway	No	
Portugal	No	
Singapore	No	
Spain	No	
Sweden	No	
Switzerland	No	
United Kingdom	No	
United States	No	No guarantee for CHIPS settlement
Armenia	No	
Belarus	n.a.	
Bulgaria	No	
China	Yes	
Czech Republic	No	
Hungary	No	
Latvia	No	
Poland	No	
Russia	No	Except in case of fraud where the central bank provides guarantee
Slovakia	No	
Slovenia	No	
Tanzania	Yes	Implicit
Vietnam	n.a.	

Central Bank Settlement Failure Guarantee (Continued)

Country	*Exists*	*Comments*
Bahrain	No	
Barbados	Yes	Central bank provides cover payments if commercial banks cannot honour obligations
Bermuda	No	
Botswana	Yes	Nonfunded positions are settled by either borrowing from the open market or by borrowing from the central bank and discounting holdings of central bank certificates
Brazil	Yes	Central bank ensures continuation of the settlement chain and has legal authority and moral suasion to charge the defaulting party
Colombia	No	
Cyprus	n.a.	Considered to be negligible
Eastern Caribbean	Yes	Implicit guarantee of Eastern Caribbean Central Bank (ECCB) by underwriting credit exposures on itself and supporting liquidity in the banking system
Egypt	No	
Fiji	No	
Guyana	No	
Jordan	No	
Kenya	No	
Korea	No	
Kuwait	Yes	Implicit
Lebanon	No	
Malawi	Yes	Implicit
Malaysia	Yes	Implicit
Malta	No	
Mauritius	No	
Mexico	No	
Morocco	Yes	Implicit
Mozambique	No	
Namibia	Yes	Implicit
Nigeria	No	
Pakistan	No	
Peru	Yes	Explicit
Saudi Arabia	No	
South Africa	Yes	See Appendix 4
Swaziland	No	
Tonga	No	
Turkey	No	
Uganda	No	
United Arab Emirates	No	
Zambia	No	Banks must maintain sufficient settlement balances at all times
Zimbabwe	n.a.	

Appendix 6

Payment System Development Strategies

(1: Evolutionary 2: Leapfrogging 3: Not applicable)

Country	*Type*	*Comments*
Australia	1	Aims at increasing soundness, reliability and efficiency (RTGS in 1998); central bank to be given formal powers to achieve these goals
Austria	3	
Belgium	3	
Canada	1	Canadian Payment Association (CPA) mandate is to establish and operate a national clearing and settlement system; CPA deals mainly with standards and rules; rapid technological advances have focused attention on new means of electronic payments
Finland	1	Gradual improvement in risk management and efficiency of the payment system
France	3	
Germany	3	
Greece	1	Involvement of the central bank in the implementation of RTGS and improvement of DNS to satisfy European Union (EU) criteria
Hong Kong	1	Efforts now concentrated on retail payments and links with securities settlement
Iceland	1	Central bank in process of implementing an RTGS
Italy	3	
Netherlands	3	
New Zealand	1	After RTGS implementation, risk reduction in the net end-of-day retail system is a priority together with foreign exchange settlement risk
Norway	3	
Portugal	2	Always favoured advanced technology
Singapore	1	Plan to move from DNS to RTGS (MEPS) in which all intraday borrowing will be collateralised
Spain	2	Spanish system has developed very recently and has incorporated the latest technology from the outset
Sweden	3	
Switzerland	3	
United Kingdom	3	
United States	3	

Payment System Development Strategies (Continued)
(*1: Evolutionary 2: Leapfrogging 3: Not applicable*)

Country	*Type*	*Comments*
Armenia	1	Development of RTGS since 1995 plus creation of national plastic card payment system
Belarus	1	Implementation of RTGS, shortening of document turnover time, improve safety and security of information and develop more efficient use of funds
Bulgaria	1	RTGS (SIC-type) to be fully achieved by 1999
China	1	China National Advanced Payment System (CNAPS) project started in 1991 with the aim of building on earlier success of Electronic Interbank System project
Czech Republic	2	Strategic decision in 1989 to use the latest technology
Hungary	2	1996 formulation of a strategy aiming at introducing RTGS without commercial bank cooperation; would like to include the commercial banks in the future
Latvia	1	Strategy based on aligning with best EU practice
Poland	1	
Russia	1	Aim is to achieve a fully centralised RTGS payment system with direct participation of commercial banks; the central bank does not intend to participate directly in netting and credit card clearing systems
Slovakia	1	Following developments in the EU closely
Slovenia	1	Implementation of RTGS bulk payment subsystem for retail credits and debits being developed; the central bank will replace the Payments Agency in the settlement procedure
Tanzania	2	Drawing on best practice abroad
Vietnam	1	

Payment System Development Strategies (Continued)
(1: Evolutionary 2: Leapfrogging 3: Not applicable)

Country	*Type*	*Comments*
Bahrain	1	Plan to share a network of automated teller machines (ATM)s with all Gulf countries
Barbados	1	
Bermuda	3	
Botswana	1	Participating in the South African Development Community (SADC) Payment System Project
Brazil	1	The focus is moving from efficiency improvements to risk reduction measures
Colombia	1	
Cyprus	1	Future implementation of RTGS being studied
Eastern Caribbean	2	1997 review recommended leapfrog strategy for small-value and personal payments
Egypt	2	Central bank is planning to reform its payment system and is planning to leapfrog to the latest technology
Fiji	1	
Guyana	1	Payment system reform project underway and expected to be completed by 2000
Jordan	1	
Kenya	1	Attention currently focused on automation of the cheque clearing system
Korea	1	Since the late 1970s, increasing emphasis on security and risk management
Kuwait	1	Automation of existing deferred *gross* settlement to be followed by introduction of RTGS
Lebanon	2	RTGS implementation planned in 1998 together with technical enhancements to improve interbank transfers
Malawi	1	National Payments Council (NPC) established to encourage the use of noncash payment instruments
Malaysia	1	Developing RTGS and ACH capabilities
Malta	1	Central bank is ensuring that new developments conform to international standards
Mauritius	2	Central bank actively considering RTGS
Mexico	1	
Morocco	1	Gradually developing from a highly cash-dominated system
Mozambique	1	Uniform Cheque Law review and respective regulation

Payment System Development Strategies (Continued)
(1: Evolutionary 2: Leapfrogging 3: Not applicable)

Country	*Type*	*Comments*
Namibia	1	Aligning Namibian payment system with the Southern African Development Community (SADC) initiative
Nigeria	1	Long-term objective is migration from cash to electronic modes of payment/settlement
Pakistan	1	Private sector body National Institutional Facilitation Technology (NIFT) is charged with automating cheque clearing process
Peru	1	National Payment Council (NPC) has been formed; cheque clearing house is to be managed by the banks
Saudi Arabia	2	Has adopted a "top down" strategy to leapfrog from cash to electronic payments
South Africa	1	National payment system project launched in 1994 with publication of the framework and strategy document (after 18-month study) focusing on systemic risk reduction, legal framework and management/governance issues
Swaziland	1	Payment system strategy is in line with Southern African Development Community (SADC) initiative
Tonga	n.a.	
Turkey	1	Successful development of multifaceted RTGS now being followed by cheque truncation initiative
Uganda	1	Existing systems being reviewed under collaborative approach that will probably include a new National Payment System Council
United Arab Emirates	2	To the latest technology
Zambia	1	Though underdeveloped banking system may influence rate of progress
Zimbabwe	1	Following the introduction of the Banking Sector Reform programme, the central bank has initiated the National Payment System Project launched at the end of 1997

Appendix 7

Separate Accounts for Required Reserves

Country	*Exists*	*Comments*
Australia	No	Settlement account balances form part of the Prime Assets Requirement (PAR)
Austria	No	
Belgium	n.a.	
Canada	n.a.	Zero reserve requirement regime
Finland	No	The reserve amount is either in the current account of the bank at the central bank or (if the bank does not have one) in a special minimum reserve account
France	No	
Germany	No	
Greece	Yes	
Hong Kong	n.a.	
Iceland	Yes	
Italy	No	
Netherlands	No	
New Zealand	No	
Norway	n.a.	
Portugal	No	
Singapore	No	
Spain	No	
Sweden	n.a.	
Switzerland	No	
United Kingdom	n.a.	
United States	No	
Armenia	No	
Belarus	n.a.	
Bulgaria	No	
China	Yes	Commercial banks hold reserves in the local branch of the central bank
Czech Republic	Yes	
Hungary	No	
Latvia	No	
Poland	No	
Russia	Yes	
Slovakia	Yes	Required reserves held in a minimum obligatory reserves account
Slovenia	Yes	
Tanzania	Yes	
Vietnam	No	

Separate Accounts for Required Reserves (Continued)

Country	*Exists*	*Comments*
Bahrain	Yes	
Barbados	Yes	
Bermuda	n.a.	
Botswana	Yes	
Brazil	Yes	Reserve requirements on time and savings deposits
Colombia	No	
Cyprus	Yes	Minimum reserve account
Eastern Caribbean	No	
Egypt	No	
Fiji	Yes	
Guyana	No	
Jordan	Yes	
Kenya	No	
Korea	n.a.	
Kuwait	n.a.	
Lebanon	No	
Malawi	Yes	Liquid Reserve Requirement accounts
Malaysia	Yes	
Malta	No	Reserves are hold in the call account at the central bank
Mauritius	No	
Mexico	No	
Morocco	No	
Mozambique	Yes	
Namibia	Yes	
Nigeria	Yes	
Pakistan	Yes	
Peru	n.a.	
Saudi Arabia	Yes	
South Africa	Yes	
Swaziland	Yes	
Tonga	Yes	
Turkey	Yes	
Uganda	No	
United Arab Emirates	Yes	
Zambia	n.a.	
Zimbabwe	Yes	

Appendix 8

Reserve Maintenance Periods

Country	*Length*	*Comments*
Australia	At all times	
Austria	Monthly	Average of the close of daily business positions registered between the first and last day of the reporting month
Belgium	n.a.	
Canada	n.a.	
Finland	Monthly	The reserve requirement is calculated against the reserve base on the last day of a calendar month and must be met during the second calendar month; daily balance can be negative up to amount of affiliates' reserve balances
France	Monthly	Average of daily balances from the 16th to the 15th of the next month
Germany	Monthly	Average of daily balances from the 16th to the 15th of the next month
Greece	Monthly	
Hong Kong	n.a.	
Iceland	Monthly	
Italy	Monthly	Average of daily balances from 15th to 14th of next month
Netherlands	Monthly	Period ends on last Thursday of the month
New Zealand	n.a.	
Norway	n.a.	
Portugal	Weekly	
Singapore	Weekly	Liability base is measured on a daily two-week basis, while Minimum Cash Balance maintenance is average weekly amount of daily balances, which can vary on any day within a 1 percent band either side of the required level
Spain	Two weeks	
Sweden	n.a.	
Switzerland	Monthly	From the 20th to the 19th of the next month
United Kingdom	n.a.	
United States	Two weeks	Period ends every other Wednesday with the average deposit base calculated over the two-week period ending on the Monday two days earlier

Reserve Maintenance Periods (Continued)

0*Country*	*Length*	*Comments*
Armenia	Two weeks	
Belarus	n.a.	
Bulgaria	Monthly	
China	Two weeks	
Czech Republic	Two weeks	Together with compulsory end-of-day balance requirement
Hungary	Two weeks	If the bank does not fulfil the requirements the central bank places the shortfall in a separate non-interest bearing account
Latvia	Monthly	
Poland	Monthly	
Russia	n.a.	
Slovakia	Monthly	Based on two two-week periods
Slovenia	Daily	
Tanzania	Daily	
Vietnam	Monthly	

Reserve Maintenance Periods (Continued)

Country	*Length*	*Comments*
Bahrain	Monthly	
Barbados	Weekly	
Bermuda	n.a.	
Botswana	Daily	
Brazil	Weekly	
Colombia	15 days	
Cyprus	n.a.	
Eastern Caribbean	Weekly	
Egypt	Weekly	
Fiji	Monthly	Starting on fifth working day
Guyana	Weekly	Thursday to Wednesday
Jordan	Weekly	
Kenya	14 days	From Thursday to following Wednesday together with a minimum requirement of 12 percent at all times
Korea	n.a.	
Kuwait	n.a.	
Lebanon	Weekly	
Malawi	Monthly	
Malaysia	Two weeks	
Malta	Monthly	
Mauritius	Weekly	
Mexico	Monthly	Zero target
Morocco	Monthly	
Mozambique	Three months	
Namibia	Monthly	
Nigeria	Monthly	
Pakistan	Weekly	
Peru	n.a.	
Saudi Arabia	Monthly	Ratio applied at the end of the month and calculation performed in the middle of the following month
South Africa	Monthly	Average of daily balances from 15th to 14th of next month
Swaziland	Daily	
Tonga	End of month	
Turkey	Weekly	
Uganda	Two weeks	The daily position is not allowed to fall below 50 percent of the minimum average required reserves for the period
United Arab Emirates	Six days	
Zambia	n.a.	
Zimbabwe	Weekly	

Appendix 9

Use of Required Reserves for Payment Purposes

Country	*Allowed*	*Comments*
Australia	Yes	Automatic rollover of intraday repo to overnight repo is allowed at penalty rate
Austria	Yes	
Belgium	n.a.	
Canada	n.a.	
Finland	Yes	Provided the monthly average of the daily current account balances meets the minimum reserve requirement
France	Yes	
Germany	Yes	
Greece	Yes	Not exceeding 10 percent of required reserves
Hong Kong	n.a.	
Iceland	No	
Italy	Yes	10 percent of required reserves may be used on an intraday basis only, while an additional 12.5 percent may be used on a daily basis
Netherlands	Yes	
New Zealand	n.a.	But commercial banks hold substantial stocks of prime liquid assets that can be used as intraday liquidity in the RTGS system
Norway	n.a.	
Portugal	Yes	
Singapore	Yes	But reserve requirements must be satisfied at the end of each day
Spain	Yes	Commercial banks can use required reserves for payments operations, so liquidity pressures are shifted to the last day of each ten-day period
Sweden	n.a.	
Switzerland	Yes	
United Kingdom	n.a.	
United States	Yes	

Use of Required Reserves for Payment Purposes (Continued)

Country	*Allowed*	*Comments*
Armenia	Yes	
Belarus	n.a.	
Bulgaria	Yes	Up to 50 percent of required reserves with penalty rate charged for use in excess of 50 percent
China	Yes	
Czech Republic	Yes	Provided end-of-day reserve requirements are maintained
Hungary	Yes	All required reserves may be used for intraday payment purposes
Latvia	Yes	
Poland	Yes	
Russia	No	
Slovakia	No	
Slovenia	Yes	Partially
Tanzania	Yes	Provided the minimum required reserves are redeposited before the Strategic Minimum Reserve reporting time
Vietnam	Yes	
Bahrain	No	
Barbados	Yes	
Bermuda	n.a.	
Botswana	No	
Brazil	Yes	
Colombia	Yes	
Cyprus	Yes	
Eastern Caribbean	Yes	
Egypt	Yes	

Use of Required Reserves for Payment Purposes (Continued)

Country	*Allowed*	*Comments*
Fiji	Yes	Provided required reserves do not fall more than 2 percent below the required level
Guyana	Yes	Provided reserve requirements are satisfied at the end of each maintenance period
Jordan	Yes	Not exceeding 20 percent of required reserves
Kenya	Yes	
Korea	n.a.	
Kuwait	n.a.	
Lebanon	Yes	
Malawi	Yes	But banks face penalties if required liquidity ratios are not satisfied
Malaysia	Yes	A bank whose clearing account at the central bank is overdrawn can borrow from another bank in surplus or can use its statutory reserve account up to a certain limit; ultimately, the central bank will meet any remaining shortfall
Malta	Yes	As long as the minimum average required reserve ratio is satisfied
Mauritius	Yes	In no case should the account be overdrawn
Mexico	n.a.	
Morocco	Yes	
Mozambique	No	
Namibia	No	In the future, banks will be able to use them within certain limits
Nigeria	No	
Pakistan	Yes	But end-of-day reserves should not be less than the minimum required
Peru	n.a.	
Saudi Arabia	No	
South Africa	Yes	Following introduction of SAMOS, banks can use their required cash reserves for intraday purposes
Swaziland	Yes	
Tonga	No	
Turkey	No	
Uganda	Yes	
United Arab Emirates	Yes	But any failure to meet the reserve requirement will attract a penalty
Zambia	n.a.	
Zimbabwe	No	

Appendix 10

Interest Paid on Reserves

Country	*Exists*	*Comments*
Australia	Yes	Monetary policy rate minus 25 basis points
Austria	No	
Belgium	n.a.	
Canada	No	
Finland	Yes	Excess reserves are remunerated at tender rate minus 200 basis points
France	No	
Germany	No	
Greece	Yes	Currently 11 percent on half the balance
Hong Kong	n.a.	
Iceland	Yes	
Italy	Yes	4.5 percent on required reserves and 0.5 percent on excess reserves
Netherlands	Yes	3.05 percent (almost equal to rates on fixed and special advances)
New Zealand	n.a.	
Norway	n.a.	
Portugal	No	
Singapore	No	
Spain	No	
Sweden	No	
Switzerland	No	
United Kingdom	No	
United States	No	
Armenia	No	
Belarus	n.a.	
Bulgaria	No	
China	Yes	5.22 percent
Czech Republic	No	
Hungary	Yes	12 percent
Latvia	No	
Poland	No	
Russia	No	
Slovakia	Yes	1.5 percent on required reserves only
Slovenia	Yes	1 percent
Tanzania	No	
Vietnam	Yes	0.2 percent per month for local currency deposits

Interest Paid on Reserves (Continued)

Country	*Exists*	*Comments*
Bahrain	No	
Barbados	No	
Bermuda	n.a.	
Botswana	No	
Brazil	Yes	Only on reserves relating to savings and time deposits
Colombia	No	
Cyprus	Yes	6 percent
Eastern Caribbean	No	
Egypt	No	
Fiji	Yes	At a rate equivalent to the yield on 91-day central bank promissory notes
Guyana	No	
Jordan	No	
Kenya	No	
Korea	n.a.	
Kuwait	n.a.	
Lebanon	No	
Malawi	Yes	5 percent on 14 percent of reserve requirement
Malaysia	No	
Malta	Yes	Currently 2.7 percent
Mauritius	No	
Mexico	No	
Morocco	No	
Mozambique	No	
Namibia	No	
Nigeria	No	
Pakistan	No	
Peru	n.a.	
Saudi Arabia	No	
South Africa	Yes	0.5 percent below treasury bill tender rate
Swaziland	No	
Tonga	No	
Turkey	No	
Uganda	No	
United Arab Emirates	No	
Zambia	No	
Zimbabwe	No	

Appendix 11

Formal Central Bank Supervision of Payment Systems

Country	*Exists*	*Comments*
Australia	Yes	Following 1997 Financial System Inquiry, a Payment Systems (Regulation) Bill is now being enacted
Austria	No	Although latest National Bank Act requires central bank to "provide support"
Belgium	No	The possibility of formal oversight is under review
Canada	Yes	Through the Payment Clearing and Settlement Act, the Bank of Canada has formal oversight role
Finland	Yes	Through the Bank of Finland Act
France	Yes	Central Bank Statute, Article 4; central bank is a major shareholder and has veto right on payment system decisions
Germany	Yes	Bundesbank Act
Greece	Yes	Law 2548 of 19 December 1997
Hong Kong	Yes	
Iceland	No	
Italy	Yes	Article 146 of 1993 Banking Law; 1997 White Paper sets guiding principles
Netherlands	Yes	Based on 1948 Bank Act; new legislation planned
New Zealand	No	
Norway	Yes	A 1996 report proposed a formal framework for payment system supervision
Portugal	Yes	Article 20 of central bank's organic law
Singapore	Yes	
Spain	Yes	Autonomy Act, 1994; Royal Decree 1369, 1987; Act of July 1988
Sweden	Yes	General provisions in Riksbank Act
Switzerland	Yes	Article 2 of the National Bank Act
United Kingdom	No	Though central bank's interests are recognised
United States	Yes	Through Federal Reserve Regulations and Policy Statements

Formal Central Bank Supervision of Payment Systems (Continued)

Country	*Exists*	*Comments*
Armenia	Yes	
Belarus	Yes	Various laws and regulatory documents
Bulgaria	Yes	Through banking law and Bulgarian National Bank Law
China	Yes	For systems owned by People's Bank of China (PBC)
Czech Republic	Yes	1993 National Bank Act
Hungary	Yes	National Bank of Hungary Act
Latvia	Yes	Bank of Latvia Act, Article 9
Poland	Yes	National Bank of Poland Act, but some systems are owned by the commercial banks
Russia	Yes	Laws on the Central Bank of Russia: Articles 3, 4 and 80
Slovakia	Yes	Oversight role of central bank established in National Bank of Slovakia (NBS) Act No. 566/1992; main laws governing payment systems are Banking Act No. 21, Notice of NBS Principles No. 275 and Bill of Exchange and Cheque Act No. 191/1950
Slovenia	Yes	Central bank approves regulations and procedures issued by the Payment Agency
Tanzania	No	
Vietnam	Yes	Law of State Bank 1997, Article 5
Bahrain	Yes	
Barbados	No	
Bermuda	No	
Botswana	No	
Brazil	Yes	Mixture of formal and informal
Colombia	Yes	Law 31, 1992
Cyprus	No	
Eastern Caribbean	Yes	Under ECCB Agreement
Egypt	Yes	Banking Law No. 163 1957 (revised)
Fiji	No	
Guyana	Yes	Bank of Guyana Act 1997, section 61
Jordan	Yes	
Kenya	No	
Korea	Yes	Bank of Korea Act
Kuwait	Yes	
Lebanon	Yes	Code of Money and Credit together with central bank circulars
Malawi	Yes	No specific law relating to payment systems but, under Reserve Bank of Malawi Act, the central bank is mandated to promote sound financial structure; National Payments Council is developing proposals for specific law on payments

Formal Central Bank Supervision of Payment Systems (Continued)

Country	*Exists*	*Comments*
Malaysia	Yes	Central Bank of Malaysia Act 1958 together with Banking and Financial Institutions Act 1989 and Bills of Exchange Act 1950
Malta	No	
Mauritius	Yes	Section 21 of the Mauritius Act 1966 provides that central bank may organise a clearing house together with banks
Mexico	Yes	Banco de México Act 1993
Morocco	Yes	
Mozambique	Yes	Sub-law no. 13 of 28 July 1994 from central bank
Namibia	Yes	Bank of Namibia Act 15, 1997, together with clearing house rules
Nigeria	Yes	Central Bank of Nigeria Decree 1991 together with Clearing House Rules
Pakistan	Yes	State Bank of Pakistan Act 1956 provides for central bank regulation of clearing houses
Peru	Yes	
Saudi Arabia	Yes	Banking Control Law 1966; SAMA also operates all payment systems
South Africa	No	Although South African Reserve Bank Act 1989 provides in general terms for central bank to organise payment systems
Swaziland	No	
Tonga	No	
Turkey	No	Although TIC-RTGS is owned and controlled by the central bank and, under the Central Bank of Turkey law, the central bank supervises the operations of cheque clearing houses
Uganda	Yes	
United Arab Emirates	Yes	Federal law plus central bank circulars
Zambia	No	
Zimbabwe	No	

Appendix 12

Informal Central Bank Supervision of Payment Systems

Country	*Exists*	*Comments*
Australia	No	
Austria	Yes	Becoming more formal (see Appendix 11)
Belgium	Yes	But see Appendix 11
Canada	Yes	Senior official of Bank of Canada is chairperson of Board of CPA; Bank of Canada also on CPA committees and working groups and has good working relationship with clearing organisations
Finland	No	
France	Yes	"Interbancarité" tradition which entrusts the central bank with a leading role in standardising banking activities
Germany	Yes	In cooperation with the banking sector
Greece	No	
Hong Kong	No	
Iceland	Yes	
Italy	Yes	Promotion of cooperation between participants, particularly in retail systems
Netherlands	No	
New Zealand	Yes	No statutory jurisdiction but a mandate to advise the government on the financial system
Norway	Yes	Currently no separate statutory regulation, so systems are regulated primarily by agreement between participants
Portugal	No	
Singapore	No	
Spain	No	
Sweden	Yes	Regular discussions
Switzerland	No	
United Kingdom	Yes	Recognition of central bank's responsibility for maintenance of financial stability
United States	No	
Armenia	No	
Belarus	No	
Bulgaria	No	
China	Yes	For systems owned by commercial banks
Czech Republic	No	
Hungary	No	
Latvia	No	
Poland	No	
Russia	No	
Slovakia	No	
Slovenia	No	
Tanzania	Yes	
Vietnam	No	

Informal Central Bank Supervision of Payment Systems (Continued)

Country	*Exists*	*Comments*
Bahrain	No	
Barbados	Yes	
Bermuda	Yes	
Botswana	Yes	Mixture of formal and informal supervision
Brazil	Yes	
Colombia	No	
Cyprus	Yes	
Eastern Caribbean	No	
Egypt	No	
Fiji	Yes	
Guyana	No	
Jordan	No	
Kenya	Yes	
0Korea	No	
Kuwait	No	
Lebanon	No	
Malawi	No	
Malaysia	No	
Malta	Yes	Central Bank of Malta Act 1967 mentions the objective of ensuring a sound financial structure
Mauritius	No	
Mexico	No	
Morocco	No	
Mozambique	Yes	
Namibia	No	
Nigeria	No	
Pakistan	No	
Peru	No	
Saudi Arabia	No	
South Africa	Yes	See Appendix 11
Swaziland	Yes	
Tonga	Yes	
Turkey	Yes	See Appendix 11
Uganda	No	
United Arab Emirates	No	
Zambia	Yes	Payment system reforms will aim to make it formal
Zimbabwe	Yes	Formal powers are to be introduced as part of the National Payment Systems Project

Appendix 13

Commercial Bank Involvement in Payment Systems

Country	*Exists*	*Comments*
Australia	Yes	Cooperation with Australian Payment Clearing Association (APCA)
Austria	Yes	
Belgium	Yes	
Canada	Yes	Commercial banks fully involved as members of the CPA
Finland	Yes	Cooperation with the Finnish Bankers' Association
France	Yes	Central bank and 11 banks participate in the Interbank Settlement Committee (CRI) which provides technical platform for TBF and SNP
Germany	Yes	Highly involved in the development of an automated and efficient banking system
Greece	Yes	Through the Hellenic Bank Association (HBA)
Hong Kong	Yes	Through involvement of Hong Kong Association of Banks (HKAB)
Iceland	Yes	RTGS being developed in cooperation with the commercial banks
Italy	Yes	Through Italian Bankers' Association
Netherlands	Yes	For example, development of improved links between the national ACH and the postal giro system
New Zealand	Yes	Often the primary initiator
Norway	Yes	Especially in cooperation for retail payment systems
Portugal	Yes	From 1983 through Interbank Services Company (SIBS) and, since 1997, through Interbank Coordinating Commission for the Retail Payment System (CISP)
Singapore	Yes	Commercial banks have played an important and supportive role in the development of the payment system
Spain	No	
Sweden	No	
Switzerland	Yes	Cooperation of the commercial banks from the beginning in the development of SIC
United Kingdom	Yes	Payment systems are privately operated with day-to-day management under the auspices of Association for Payment Clearing Services (APACS) and its three clearing companies
United States	Yes	Continuous cooperation (formal and informal) with the commercial banks

Commercial Bank Involvement in Payment Systems (Continued)

Country	*Exists*	*Comments*
Armenia	Yes	Association with major banks in solving problems
Belarus	No	
Bulgaria	Yes	Full cooperation with the commercial banks
China	Yes	Greatly involved
Czech Republic	No	Central bank is leading the process
Hungary	No	But the intention is to increase commercial bank involvement
Latvia	Yes	Consultation with the commercial banks through the National Payment Consultative Council (including the central bank, 11 commercial banks and international experts)
Poland	Yes	Joint ownership of the clearing company
Russia	No	Meetings with the commercial banks but no direct participation of commercial banks
Slovakia	Yes	Banks as shareholders of SNCC are directly involved in the changes being made
Slovenia	Yes	Not all the banks are involved
Tanzania	Yes	Joint ownership of the payment systems
Vietnam	No	
Bahrain	Yes	Commercial banks are owners of the domestic ATM network
Barbados	n.a.	Relatively young banking system
Bermuda	Yes	Commercial banks are forming a jointly owned company
Botswana	Yes	Clearing House Committee includes central bank and commercial banks
Brazil	No	
Colombia	Yes	Central bank and Colombian Banking Association have formed joint task force groups
Cyprus	Yes	Commercial banks operate the credit card payment system
Eastern Caribbean	n.a.	
Egypt	Yes	The commercial banks will participate in implementing the new system and they will adjust their internal systems to make them compatible
Fiji	Yes	Banks have introduced plastic card systems and, in future, will be involved in the National Payment System Committee
Guyana	Yes	Banks sit on the Operations Committee of the Payment System Reform Project
Jordan	Yes	Highly involved in the National Payment Council
Kenya	Yes	Banks are expected to acquire their own processing equipment in the cheque automation project

Commercial Bank Involvement in Payment Systems (Continued)

Country	*Exists*	*Comments*
Korea	Yes	Through Korea Financial Telecommunications and Clearings Institute (KTFC)
Kuwait	Yes	Commercial banks will be invited to participate in development of RTGS
Lebanon	Yes	Through joint working groups and Commission for Banking Technology
Malawi	Yes	Banks fully involved in National Payment System Modernisation Plan and sit on the National Payments Council
Malaysia	Yes	Close cooperation between the central bank and financial institutions to promote efficient banking services
Malta	Yes	Active and innovative role driven by cost savings
Mauritius	Yes	
Mexico	Yes	Through the Bankers' Association
Morocco	Yes	
Mozambique	Yes	
Namibia	Yes	Payment System Strategic Planning Committee formed in November 1997 involving both central bank and commercial banks
Nigeria	Yes	Banks are fully represented in the Technical Committee on the Automation of the Payment Systems
Pakistan	Yes	Commercial banks participate in NIFT (see Appendix 6)
Peru	Yes	Central bank will allow private sector to assume management of the automated clearing house
Saudi Arabia	Yes	Cooperation and competition between banks is encouraged
South Africa	Yes	Banks have fully "bought into" the national payment system project
Swaziland	Yes	Bankers' Technical Committee is participating in national payment system review
Tonga	No	
Turkey	Yes	TIC-RTGS was developed with the banks
Uganda	Yes	Future constitution of a National Payment System Council will involve both the central bank and the commercial banks
United Arab Emirates	No	
Zambia	Yes	Working committees where banks are represented (see Appendix 6)
Zimbabwe	Yes	A Strategy Formulation Group has been set up comprising central bank and commercial bank participants

Appendix 14

Exchange Rate Regimes and Monetary Policy

(A: Fixed B: Managed C: Floating)

Country	*Type*	*Comments*
Australia	C	
Austria	A	Recent change in payment system has had no major impact on monetary policy
Belgium	A	Transmission mechanism of monetary policy has not been affected by the introduction of the RTGS system; the provision of secured intraday loans does not interfere with the conduct of monetary policy
Canada	A	Introduction of LVTS will improve intraday liquidity monitoring and thereby facilitate monetary policy implementation
Finland	A	Monetary policy has not been affected by changes in the payment system
France	A	Provision of intraday liquidity in TBF has apparently had no monetary impact
Germany	A	
Greece	B	Financial innovations and the increasing use of noncash instruments may have been a factor contributing to the move from a monetary target to an exchange rate target
Hong Kong	A	Since RTGS implementation, the Hong Kong Monetary Authority (HKMA) has become the settlement agent operating directly in the interbank market to adjust liquidity; this has produced a quicker and more effective transmission mechanism for monetary policy
Iceland	A	The payment system has been the same since 1975, so no influence has been noticed as far as monetary policy is concerned
Italy	A	Reforms undertaken by the central bank have had some impact on the procedures for conducting monetary policy and have reduced volatility of overnight interest rates
Netherlands	A	Development of noncash instruments and easier substitution between assets may require new definitions of monetary aggregates and may produce higher velocity of money; impact of payment system changes on monetary policy is thought to be negligible because monetary policy does not use a monetary aggregate as an intermediate target; however, the precise impact on the transmission mechanism cannot be quantified
New Zealand	C	Introduction of RTGS system has not yet affected monetary policy implementation
Norway	B	Impact of the introduction of the new payment system on monetary policy has yet to be assessed
Portugal	A	The implementation of RTGS allows flexible injections of liquidity to meet changes in money market conditions and enables banks to reduce excess reserve holdings

Exchange Rate Regimes and Monetary Policy (Continued)
(A: Fixed B: Managed C: Floating)

Country	*Type*	*Comments*
Singapore	B	Effects on monetary policy implementation yet to be observed
Spain	A	No direct effects on monetary policy implementation observed
Sweden	C	No direct effects on monetary policy implementation observed
Switzerland	C	Introduction of RTGS in 1987, with no additional intra-day liquidity provision by the central bank, forced banks to economise on their use of reserves; this behavioural change was not recognised immediately and so led to a looser monetary policy than intended, given monetary base targeting at that time
United Kingdom	C	Change to RTGS did not cause any particular problems with respect to monetary policy implementation, although some operational adjustments have been required
United States	C	No direct implication of payment system changes for monetary policy; risk of technological failure requires the Fed to respond to temporary outflows of funds from the system
Armenia	C	As a result of developments in the payment system since 1996, noncash money and velocity of money have both increased
Belarus	C	
Bulgaria	A	Implementation of BISERA helps provide information about liquidity positions
China	B	Currently payment system operations have little impact on monetary policy implementation
Czech Republic	B	Payment system enables real-time liquidity monitoring
Hungary	B	Central bank increased reserve requirements in order to counter the potentially expansionary effect of the introduction of IGS in 1994
Latvia	B	Introduction of EFTS has accelerated interbank settlements, improved liquidity management, helped develop the money market and reduced excess reserve holdings
Poland	B	The reduced central bank float has improved liquidity management
Russia	B	
Slovakia	A	The system's construction enables effective and efficient monetary policy implementation and transmission
Slovenia	B	Changes in the payment system will allow the central bank to monitor liquidity of commercial banks and to implement the control of monetary policy

Exchange Rate Regimes and Monetary Policy (Continued)
(A: Fixed B: Managed C: Floating)

Country	*Type*	*Comments*
Tanzania	C	Effects of payment system changes not yet apparent; more is expected when the money and securities markets are in place
Vietnam	B	Share of cash in *M2* began to fall from 1994 due to the payment system modernisation
Bahrain	A	No impact on monetary policy because the central bank does not conduct open-market operations that rely on payment system channels
Barbados	A	
Bermuda	A	
Botswana	A	Modernisation of the payment system is too recent to assess implications for monetary policy implementation
Brazil	C	There have been no significant payment system changes in recent years that have affected monetary policy implementation
Colombia	B	So far changes in the payment system design have not affected monetary policy implementation
Cyprus	A	
Eastern Caribbean	A	
Egypt	B	The inefficient payment system affects adversely liquidity management both by banks and the monetary authorities as well as preventing the use of monetary instruments to implement monetary policy
Fiji	A	
Guyana	C	Increased payment efficiency will increase velocity of circulation of money; moreover, increased use of non-cash instruments will force banks to improve reserve management, so raising the effectiveness of market-based monetary control techniques
Jordan	A	Too early to assess effects of payment system modernisation on monetary policy implementation
Kenya	C	So far payment system developments have not affected adversely monetary policy
Korea	B	Payment system developments have accelerated the transmission of monetary and credit policies
Kuwait	A	No implications have been noticed yet but development of electronic cash may affect monetary policy
Lebanon	C	
Malawi	C	
Malaysia	B	
Malta	A	Central bank powers to formulate and implement monetary policy acquired in 1994 have provided an incentive to payment system development

Exchange Rate Regimes and Monetary Policy (Continued)
(A: Fixed B: Managed C: Floating)

Country	*Type*	*Comments*
Mauritius	B	Payment systems are evolving gradually with no impact so far on monetary policy implementation and transmission
Mexico	C	
Morocco	A	
Mozambique	C	
Namibia	A	
Nigeria	A	Monetary management has been improved by the reduction in float and production of accurate flow-of-funds data, but the lag in consolidation of bank reserves nationwide continues to present problems
Pakistan	B	Too early to assess effect of payment system modernisation on monetary policy implementation
Peru	C	Introduction of RTGS and full collateralisation of intraday credit will affect demand for liquidity
Saudi Arabia	A	The development of an electronic payment system allows a faster injection of liquidity in the economy, smooths the demand for overnight funds, limits fluctuations in interest rates and promotes efficient use of deposit money (i.e., increases velocity)
South Africa	C	The introduction of SAMOS will allow rapid transmission of monetary policy through interbank and short-term money markets
Swaziland	A	
Tonga	A	
Turkey	B	Introduction of new instruments in payment system affects the level and volatility of bank reserves but it remains difficult to estimate effects of changes in payment system on money transmission
Uganda	C	Improvement in the payment system should lead to a more efficient transmission mechanism of monetary policy via the central bank's operations in government and central bank securities through a well-established secondary market
United Arab Emirates	A	Once implemented, the new payment system will provide fast and accurate information that will have some influence on monetary policy
Zambia	C	Improvements to date have decreased the level of float and increased central bank control over reserve money
Zimbabwe	C	Changes likely in future following completion of National Payment System Project

Bibliography

Allsopp, Peter (1995), "Interbank Exposures in the International Payment System" (Hong Kong: Paper delivered at a Seminar on Global Payment Systems organised by the Hong Kong Monetary Authority, November).

Bagehot, Walter (1873), *Lombard Street: A Description of the Money Market* (New York: Scribner, Armstrong).

Bain, Keith and Peter G. A. Howells (1991), "The Income and Transactions Velocities of Money," *Review of Social Studies*, 49(3), Fall, pp. 383–395.

Baliño, Tomás J. T., Juhi Dhawan and Venkataraman Sundararajan (1994), "Payment System Reform and Monetary Policy in Emerging Market Economies in Central and Eastern Europe," *International Monetary Fund Staff Papers*, 41(3), September, pp. 383–395.

Bank for International Settlements (annual), *Statistics on Payment Systems in the Group of Ten Countries* (Basle: Bank for International Settlements).

——— (1989), *Statistics on Payment Systems in Eleven Developed Countries for 1988* (Basle: Bank for International Settlements, December).

——— (1990), *Report of the Committee on Interbank Netting Schemes of the Central Banks of the Group of Ten Countries (Lamfalussy Report)* (Basle: Bank for International Settlements).

——— (1993), *Payment Systems in the Group of Ten Countries* (Basle: Bank for International Settlements).

——— (1996), *Settlement Risk in Foreign Exchange Transactions* (Basle: Bank for International Settlements, March).

——— (1997*a*), *Payment Systems in Korea* (Basle: Bank for International Settlements, March).

——— (1997*b*), *Real-Time Gross Settlement Systems* (Basle: Bank for International Settlements, March).

——— (1997*c*), *Statistics on Payment Systems in the Group of Ten Countries for 1996* (Basle: Bank for International Settlements, December).

——— (1998), *Managing Change in Payment Systems* (Basle: Bank for International Settlements, BIS Policy Papers 4, May).

Bank of England (1994), "The Development of a UK Real-Time Gross Settlement System," *Bank of England Quarterly Review*, 34(2), May, pp. 163–168.

Benston, George J. and George G. Kaufman (1995), "Is the Banking and Payments System Fragile?" *Journal of Financial Services Research*, 9(3–4), December, pp. 209–240.

Berger, Allen, Diana Hancock and Jeffrey Marquardt (1996), "A Framework for Analyzing Efficiency, Risks, Costs, and Innovations in the Payments System," *Journal of Money, Credit and Banking*, 28(4, ii), November, pp. 696–732.

Blommestein, Hans J. and Bruce J. Summers (1994), "Banking and the Payment System" in *The Payment System: Design, Management, and Supervision* edited by Bruce J. Summers (Washington, DC: International Monetary Fund), pp. 15–28.

Borio, Claudio E. V. and Paul Van den Bergh (1993), "The Nature and Management of Payment System Risks: An International Perspective" (Basle: Bank for International Settlements, BIS Economic Paper 36, February).

Capie, Forrest, Charles A. E. Goodhart, Stanley Fischer and Norbert Schnadt (1994), *The Future of Central Banking: The Tercentenary Symposium of the Bank of England* (Cambridge: Cambridge University Press).

Considine, Jill M. (1995), "Risk Reduction and Enhanced Efficiency in Large-Value Payment Systems: A Private Sector Response" (Hong Kong: Paper delivered at a Seminar on Global Payment Systems organised by the Hong Kong Monetary Authority, November).

Crockett, Andrew (1998), "Welcoming Presentation" in *Managing Change in Payment Systems* (Basle: Bank for International Settlements, BIS Policy Papers 4, May), pp. 1–8.

Dale, Spencer and Marco Rossi (1996), "A Market for Intra-day Funds: Does It Have Implications for Monetary Policy?" (London: Bank of England, Working Paper Series 46, March).

Effros, Robert C., ed. (1992–1998) *Current Legal Issues Affecting Central Banks,* Volumes 1–5 (Washington, DC: International Monetary Fund).

———, ed. (1994) *Payment Systems of the World* (New York: Oceana Publications).

Federal Reserve Bank of New York (1993), *Reduced Reserve Requirements: Alternatives for the Conduct of Monetary Policy and Reserve Management* (New York: Federal Reserve Bank of New York).

Flannery, Mark J. (1996), "Financial Crises, Payment System Problems, and Discount Window Lending," *Journal of Money, Credit and Banking*, 28(4, ii), November, pp. 804–824.

Folkerts-Landau, David (1997), "Wholesale Payments and Financial Discipline, Efficiency, and Liquidity" (Washington, DC: International Monetary Fund, WP/97/154, November).

Folkerts-Landau, David, Peter Garber and Dirk Schoenmaker (1996), "The Reform of Wholesale Payment Systems and Its Impact of Financial Markets" (Washington, DC: Group of Thirty, Occasional Paper 51).

Freeman, Scott (1996*a*), "Clearinghouse Banks and Banknote Over-issue," *Journal of Monetary Economics*, 38(1), August, pp. 101–115.

Freeman, Scott (1996*b*), "The Payments System, Liquidity, and Rediscounting," *American Economic Review*, 86(5), December, pp. 1126–1138.

Freixas, Xavier and Bruno Parigi (1998), "Contagion and Efficiency in Gross and Net Interbank Payment Systems," *Journal of Financial Intermediation*, 7(1), January, pp. 3–31.

Friedman, Milton (1969), *The Optimum Quantity of Money and Other Essays* (Chicago: Aldine).

Fry, Maxwell J. (1995), *Money, Interest, and Banking in Economic Development*, 2nd edn (Baltimore: Johns Hopkins University Press).

——— (1997), *Emancipating the Banking System and Developing Markets for Government Debt* (London: Routledge).

Fry, Maxwell J., Charles A. E. Goodhart and Alvaro Almeida (1996), *Central Banking in Developing Countries: Objectives, Activities and Independence* (London: Routledge).

Goodfriend, Marvin (1990), "Money, Credit, Banking, and Payment System Policy" in *The U.S. Payment System: Efficiency, Risk and the Role of the Federal Reserve* edited by David B. Humphrey (Boston: Kluwer Academic Publishers), pp. 247–284.

Goodhart, Charles A. E. (1989), *Money, Information and Uncertainty*, 2nd edn (Basingstoke: Macmillan).

Goodhart, Charles A. E., Philipp Hartmann, David Llewellyn, Liliana Rojas-Suárez and Steven Weisbrod (1998), *Financial Regulation: Why, How and Where Now?* (London: Routledge).

Hancock, Diana and David B. Humphrey (1997), "Payment Transactions, Instruments, and Systems: A Survey," *Journal of Banking and Finance*, 21(11–12), December, pp. 1573–1624.

Hilton, Spence, Melissa Gerdts and Roxann Robinson (1993), "Paying Interest on Reserves" in *Reduced Reserve Requirements: Alternatives for the Conduct of Monetary Policy and Reserve Management by the Federal Reserve Bank of New York* (New York: Federal Reserve Bank of New York), pp. 63–108.

Holmström, Bengt and Jean Tirole (1998), "Private and Public Supply of Liquidity," *Journal of Political Economy*, 106(1), February, pp. 1–40.

Hook, Andrew T. (1995) "Payment System Policy in the Group of Ten Countries: Lesson and Implications for Economies in Transition" (Washington, DC: International Monetary Fund, March).

Howells, Peter G. A. and Khaled Hussein (1997), "The Demand for Money: Total Transactions as the Scale Variable," *Economics Letters*, 55(3), 12 September, pp. 371–377.

Howitt, Peter (1992), "Optimum Quantity of Money" in *The New Palgrave Dictionary of Money and Finance* edited by Peter Newman, Murray Milgate and John Eatwell (London: Macmillan), pp. 81–83.

Humphrey, David B. and Allen N. Berger (1990), "Market Failure and Resource Use: Economic Incentives to Use Different Payment Instruments" in *The U.S. Payment System: Efficiency, Risk and the Role of the Federal Reserve* edited by David B. Humphrey (Boston: Kluwer Academic Publishers), pp. 45–86.

Humphrey, David B., Setsuya Sato, Masayoshi Tsurumi and Jukka M. Vesala (1996), "The Evolution of Payments in Europe, Japan, and the United States: Lessons for Emerging Market Economies" (Washington, DC: World Bank, Financial Sector Development Department, Policy Research Working Paper 1676, October).

Humphrey, David B., Laurence B. Pulley and Jukka M. Vesala (1996), "Cash, Paper, and Electronic Payments: A Cross-Country Analysis," *Journal of Money, Credit and Banking*, 28(4, ii), November, pp. 914–939.

Humphrey, David B., Robert H. Keppler and Fernando Montes-Negret (1997), "Cost Recovery and Pricing of Payment Services" (Washington, DC: World Bank, Financial Sector Development Department, Policy Research Working Paper 1833, October).

Johnson, Omotunde E. G. (1998), "Payment System and Monetary Policy" (London: Bank of England, Centre for Central Banking Studies, Paper prepared for the Academic Workshop on Payment and Settlement Systems, 12–16 January).

Johnson, Omotunde E. G., Richard K. Abrams, Jean-Marc Destresse, Tony Lybek, Nicholas M. Roberts and Mark Swinburne (1998), *Payment Systems, Monetary Policy, and the Role of the Central Bank* (Washington, DC: International Monetary Fund).

Lin See Yan (1991), "Interaction of Exchange Rate Policy and Monetary Policy: The Case of Malaysia" in *Monetary Policy Instruments for Developing Countries* edited by Gerard Caprio, Jr. and Patrick Honohan (Washington, DC: World Bank), pp. 131–134.

Lindley, Robert (1998), "RTGS versus DNS: The Wrong Debate?" (London: Bank of England, Centre for Central Banking Studies, Paper prepared for the Academic Workshop on Payment and Settlement Systems, 12–16 January).

Listfield, Robert and Fernando Montes-Negret (1994), "Modernizing Payment Systems in Emerging Economies" (Washington, DC: World Bank, Financial Sector Development Department, Policy Research Working Paper 1336, August).

——— (1995), "Payment Systems in Latin America: A Tale of Two Countries: Colombia and El Salvador" (Washington, DC: World Bank, Financial Sector Development Department, Policy Research Working Paper 1519, October).

Listfield, Robert and Fernando Montes-Negret (1996), "Brazil's Efficient Payment System: A Legacy of High Inflation" (Washington, DC: World Bank, Financial Sector Development Department, Policy Research Working Paper 1680, November).

Lubke, Theo (1998), "Converting Settlement of Principal and Income Payments on Securities from Next-Day Funds to Same-Day Funds" (London: Bank of England, Centre for Central Banking Studies, Paper prepared for the Academic Workshop on Payment and Settlement Systems, 12–16 January).

McDonough, William J. (1998), "Managing Change in Payment Systems" in *Managing Change in Payment Systems* (Basle: Bank for International Settlements, BIS Policy Papers 4, May), pp. 9–17.

Markowitz, Harry M. (1959), *Portfolio Selection: Efficient Diversification of Investments* (New Haven: Yale University Press).

Patrikis, Ernest T. (1995), "Global Payment Systems: The Challenge For Central Banks" (Hong Kong: Keynote Address at a Seminar on Global Payment Systems organised by the Hong Kong Monetary Authority, November).

Pesek, Boris (1976), "Monetary Theory in the Post-Robertson 'Alice in Wonderland'," *Journal of Economic Literature*, 14(3) September, pp. 856–884.

Reain, James (1998), "Underwriting Systemic Risk" (London: Bank of England, Centre for Central Banking Studies, Paper prepared for the Academic Workshop on Payment and Settlement Systems, 12–16 January).

Sato, Setsuya and David B. Humphrey (1995), "Transforming Payment Systems: Meeting the Needs of Emerging Market Economies" (Washington, DC: World Bank, World Bank Discussion Paper 291, July).

Schoenmaker, Dirk (1995), "A Comparison of Alternative Interbank Settlement Systems" (London: London School of Economics, LSE Financial Markets Group Discussion Paper 204, March).

Sendrovic, Israel (1995), "Technology and Payment Systems" (New York: Federal Reserve Bank of New York).

Stojanovic, Aleksandar (1998), "Payment Systems Cross-Country Analysis: The Bank of England Group" (London: City University Business School, August).

Summers, Bruce J., ed. (1994), *The Payment System: Design, Management, and Supervision* (Washington, DC: International Monetary Fund).

Sundararajan, Venkataraman (1994), "Linkages between Payments Systems Reforms and Monetary Policy: The Recent Experience in Russia and Other Former Soviet Union Countries" in *Framework for Monetary Stability: Issues and Country Experiences* edited by Tomás J. T. Baliño and Carlo Cottarelli (Washington, DC: International Monetary Fund), pp. 611–654.

Tobin, James (1958), "Liquidity Preference as Behavior towards Risk," *Review of Economic Studies*, 25(2), February, pp. 65–86.

Veale, John M. and Robert W. Price (1994), "Payment System Float and Float Management" in *The Payment System: Design, Management, and Supervision edited* by Bruce J. Summers (Washington, DC: International Monetary Fund), pp. 145–163.

White, William (1998), "Payment System Change and Financial Stability" in *Managing Change in Payment Systems* (Basle: Bank for International Settlements, BIS Policy Papers 4, May), pp. 173–192.

Yam, Joseph (1998), "Enhancing Domestic and Cross-Border Payment System Arrangements to Cope with Liberalisation and Globalisation of Financial Markets" in *Managing Change in Payment Systems* (Basle: Bank for International Settlements, BIS Policy Papers 4, May), pp. 124–127.

Index

Note: Page numbers followed by *t, f* or *n* indicate material contained in tables, figures or notes, respectively.